Folktales Aloud

Folktales Aloud

Practical Advice for Playful Storytelling

JANICE M. DEL NEGRO

ala
editions

An imprint of the American Library Association
Chicago   2014

JANICE M. DEL NEGRO is an associate professor at the Graduate School of Library and Information Science at Dominican University in River Forest, Illinois, where she teaches storytelling, children's and young adult literature, and foundations of library and information science. She is also on the advisory board for the Butler Center, Dominican's new center for children's and young adult literature. Before coming to Dominican, she was the editor for *The Bulletin of the Center for Children's Books*. Her list of presentations and publications is extensive and includes a textbook on storytelling coauthored with Ellin Greene; two children's picture books, the ALA Notable Book *Willa and the Wind* and *Lucy Dove*, which won the Anne Izard Storytellers' Choice Award; and a collection of supernatural tales for young adults, *Passion and Poison*. She has served on several ALA book selection committees and is an active storyteller, having appeared at the National Storytelling Festival and similar events around the country.

© 2014 by the American Library Association.

Printed in the United States of America
18 17 16 15 14   5 4 3 2 1

Extensive effort has gone into ensuring the reliability of the information in this book; however, the publisher makes no warranty, express or implied, with respect to the material contained herein.

ISBNs: 978-0-8389-1135-8 (paper); 978-0-8389-9631-7 (PDF); 978-0-8389-9632-4 (ePub); 978-0-8389-9633-1 (Kindle). For more information on digital formats, visit the ALA Store at alastore.ala.org and select eEditions.

Library of Congress Cataloging-in-Publication Data

Del Negro, Janice M.
    Folktales aloud : practical advice for playful storytelling / Janice M. Del Negro.
        pages   cm
    Includes bibliographical references and index.
    ISBN 978-0-8389-1135-8 (alk. paper)
    1. Storytelling. 2. Children's libraries—Activity programs. 3. Elementary school libraries—Activity programs. 4. Tales. I. Title.
    Z718.3.D45 2014
    027.62'51—dc23

2013028036

Cover design by Kirstin Krutsch. Images © Shutterstock, Inc.
Text design by Kim Thornton in Adobe Garamond Pro and Scala Sans

♾ This paper meets the requirements of ANSI/NISO Z39.48-1992 (Permanence of Paper).

To my students

CONTENTS

Acknowledgments ix

1	**A Narrative Journey: A Librarian's Tale**	1

2	**Storyplay: Ages 3 to 6**	9

StoryCoaching: "The Three Billy Goats Gruff" 12

Stories for Ages 3 to 6 19

"The Great Big Enormous Turnip" *19*

"The Hungry Wolf" *21*

"The Teeny-Tiny Woman" *25*

"PLOP! Splash! A Folktale from Tibet" *27*

3	**Cooperation and Community: Ages 6 to 9**	31

StoryCoaching: "The North Wind and the Sun" 36

Stories for Ages 6 to 9 44

"The Hedley Kow" *44*

"Jack and His Comrades" *48*

"King Hairy Goat Ears" *56*

"The Monkey, the Dog, and the Carabao" *61*

4   Surprise and Laughter: Ages 9 to 12   **67**

StoryCoaching: "Tailypo, a Jump Tale" 73

Stories for Ages 9 to 12 82

   "Four Friends and a Lion" *82*

   "Liver" *85*

   "The Demon Goblin of Adachigahara" *89*

   "To Your Good Health!" *94*

5   Intensity and Honor: Ages 12 to 14   **103**

StoryCoaching: "Mr. Fox" 107

Stories for Ages 12 to 14 116

   "A Ghost Story" *116*

   "Clever Grethel" *122*

   "The Magic Pipe: A Norse Tale" *126*

   "The Wild Geese" *140*

6   Beyond the Legacy: Storytelling Now   **149**

References and Resources

   Resources for Researching Folktales and Storytelling 157

   Storytelling How-and-Why Books 161

   Folktale Picture Books 165

   Folktale Collections 179

   Stories and Storytelling on the Web 195

   Index 199

ACKNOWLEDGMENTS

***Folktales Aloud* is an offering** to those who love and promote story-telling in all its diversity, especially those who have promoted storytelling in school and public libraries for the last 120-odd years. They were and are librarians, storytellers, collectors, teachers, and scholars, and this book stands on the foundation they created. These individuals—LeClaire Alger, Augusta Baker, Pura Belpré, Frances Eunice Bowman, Sara Cone Bryant, Mary Gould Davis, Virginia Haviland, Alice Kane, Elizabeth Nesbitt, Frances Jenkins Olcott, Margaret Poarch, Effie Louise Power, Charlemae Hill Rollins, Ruth Sawyer, Frances Clarke Sayers, Marie Shedlock—held the raw flame of story in their hands and passed it on to the librarian storytellers who came after them—Carol Birch, Sue Black, Milbre Burch, Gail de Vos, Elizabeth Ellis, Irene Fahrenwald, Elizabeth Figa, Ellin Greene, Mary Hamilton, Janice Harrington, Betsy Hearne, Steve Herb, Beth Horner, Sujin Huggins, Jim Jeske, Ron Jones, Melanie Kimball, Maggie Kimmel, Michael Leonard, Margaret Read MacDonald, Kate McDowell, Lee McLain,

Mary Ogilvie, Anne Pellowski, Marie Ringenberg, Anne Shimojima, John Stewig, Janet Thompson, and many, many others. There is no way to include the names of all those who deserve to be thanked; please know that my gratitude extends to all those librarian storytellers who told and continue to tell stories to those in their charge. Special thanks to my graduate assistant Emily Fardoux for her enthusiastic tenacity, and to my dean, Susan Roman, for her constant encouragement. This book would be a wisp in the dark without editor Stephanie Zvirin, who has the patience of a saint.

CHAPTER 1

A NARRATIVE JOURNEY

A Librarian's Tale

I took a storytelling class in graduate library school. Not because I wanted to, but because it was expected that anyone planning on going into youth services in the school or public library would do so. I was terrified. I hated public speaking of any kind and spent most of the semester in a state of stomach-roiling panic.

When I got my first job as a children's librarian at the Chicago Public Library, I was lucky enough to be taken under the wings of two experienced youth services librarians, Dorothy Evans and Grace O'Connor. These wise women helped me navigate the sea of programming that was expected of the successful children's librarian and kept me from drowning in preschool storytimes and other events. My most important lessons, however, came from the children to whom I told stories.

My fear of public speaking did not disappear when I became a professional children's librarian, but I found if I could keep other grown-ups out of preschool storytime, my fears were greatly assuaged. After all, the children (ages 3 to 5 years old) didn't care; they were happy to participate in whatever program I managed to put together. Despite having taken a storytelling class, and despite having the advice of other librarians, my early programs with preschoolers tended more toward maintaining control and less toward communicating the joy of story. I believed (because that's what I was told in library school) that preschoolers needed the visual stimulus of the picture book in order to connect to story, and so my programs were locked into a certain standard, albeit successful, way of doing things: an opening song, a picture book, an action rhyme or fingerplay, another picture book, another action rhyme or fingerplay, a final picture book, a closing chant or song. The programs were solid, and they did what they were supposed to do: children loved the books, loved chanting and singing, loved the routine, and as a result checked out lots of books, which made everyone very happy. The circulation numbers were up, the program attendance statistics were high, and parents with children in preschool storytime were reading aloud at home sometimes far in excess of the recommended twenty minutes a day.

I was, however, unsatisfied. The manner of presentation quickly became rote, the presentation of programs a chore instead of a joy. I had attended a number of storytelling festivals, and I knew that a different sort of storytelling was possible, at least with older listeners. Still, there was that edict from library school: preschoolers need the visual stimulus of the picture book.

One day I sat in preschool storytime, twenty-five preschoolers gathered around my feet, as I read, once again, Paul Galdone's *The Three Billy Goats Gruff*. By now I had read this story so many times (the children loved it, and who was I to deprive them?) that I knew where the page turns were without even looking. As I told the story, daylight slowly dawned: the children, twenty-five nearly always squiggly preschoolers sitting attentively on the floor, were not looking at the book at all; they were looking at my face as I told the tale. At that moment I did a very dangerous thing; I closed the book, and, as a popular penguin cartoon character once did, I departed from the text. I told the story without the book. Putting the book down meant I could use my hands to more effectively communicate; I could look at each and every child as I told. The complex and sometimes exasperating logistics of holding the book so everyone could see were eliminated; everyone could see without difficulty because now the pictures were in their imaginations. As the story went on the children scooted up toward my chair, until they were clustered closely around my feet, some even holding on to the hem of my pants. When we got to the end of the story, the cries of "Again! Do it again!" motivated me to do something additionally radical. I decided we would act it out.

An aside is necessary here. Have you ever read books about creative dramatics? I have. The older titles I read seemed determined to make what is essentially a very simple activity into something more complicated than it needs to be. Some of those books on creative dramatics were short on both the creative and the dramatic and long on the concept of controlling the group. Because I had already put aside the idea that preschoolers needed the picture book for visual stimulation, I decided to toss caution to the wind, give up my desire to control the group, and just see what happened. We acted out "The Three Billy Goats Gruff" with three goats and a troll (my chair was the bridge); the remaining preschoolers served as a sort of chorus for the refrains and sound effects. I was the narrator, director, and encourager, chanting the words and maneuvering the action. The energy was palpable, the program joyously rowdy, the children thoroughly engaged in the language and the action. When giving out books at the end of the program—I always give out books at the end of a program—one 4-year-old boy said, "Let's do 'The Three Little Pigs' next week!" "Sure," I said—and promptly forgot about it.

The following week preschool storytime rolled around. I did a newly energized program that included a highly successful participatory version of "The Great Big Enormous Turnip" and prepared to release my charges back into the children's room, when that 4-year-old boy looked at me with big eyes and said, "You promised we'd do 'The Three Little Pigs.'" There is a special very hot place within another very hot place for a children's librarian who breaks a promise to a 4-year-old, so, despite the fact that storytime was essentially over, I took a deep breath and began. There was only one problem: I did not really know the story of "The Three Little Pigs." Oh, I knew the general gist of the tale, but really, my strongest memory of the story was the Walt Disney movie: it was the only movie we had at my previous library, and we showed it all the time. Having already thrown caution to the wind the previous week, I told my preschoolers that they would have to help, and we, very seriously, went about the process of assigning parts (why is it that the quietest child always wants to be the villain?) with the unfeatured remaining children getting a choral refrain so everyone was included. I was the narrator—also the doors to the houses of straw, twigs, and bricks. I stood, with the first little pig standing behind me, as the wolf (a very proper little girl with a very proper little bow) pounded on my hands, saying, "Little pig, little pig, let me come in!" Before I could say a word, the first little pig popped out from behind me and said sassily, "Not by the hair of my chinny chin chin!" We were off.

Each time the wolf huffed and puffed, a little pig escaped to the next house, until finally all three little pigs were in the house of bricks. Up on the roof: "He was big, he was bad, he was ugly. He was the big bad wolf, and he was going down the chimney to eat the Three Little Pigs!" There was a collective gasp from the assembled children. "But the third little pig was a smart little pig. She put a big pot of boiling water on the fire, and when the wolf came down the chimney, into the pot he went! She clapped on the lid and the Three Little Pigs had wolf stew for lunch!" Twenty-five preschoolers burst into spontaneous applause. Their mothers, who had been peeking into the storytime room to see what was taking so long, were laughing both at their children's obvious enjoyment and at their dramatic antics. It was a professional epiphany. I had read many articles that talked about how preschoolers learn through play, many articles about the power of story to hold a group and create community, many articles about how folktales were the most effective form of narrative to use with children, but no article, no book, could have taught me what I learned that day from twenty-five preschoolers: the sublime and wonderful joy of playing with story.

Storytelling in the library and school setting can take many forms. For the purposes of this book, storytelling is the oral presentation of narrative to a group of listeners, face-to-face, in real time, without text or props. This book is even more specific in that the narrative being presented is the folktale, another term that can have many definitions, depending on whether you are a librarian, folklorist, or sociopolitical activist. Again, for the purposes of this book, traditional folktales are very basically defined as stories once passed on orally from generation to generation, now captured on the page, waiting to be passed on orally once again. These stories can include fairy tales, myths, legends, and other forms of orally transmitted narrative.

The popular folktale most often has an obvious structure that makes it easy to learn, simple to tell, and enjoyable to hear. Sheila Dailey's excellent book, *Putting the World in a Nutshell: The Art of the Formula Tale*, discusses the characteristic structure of the basic formula folktale.

The best way to find stories to tell is to explore the folktales already on the shelf in your school or public library. The more familiar you are with the available body of folktales for youth, the more expert and discriminating you will become at selecting stories for telling. Folktales have been an integral part of juvenile library collections since the turn of the twentieth century, and there is a long history of telling folktales to children of all ages in both schools and libraries. The process is a rewarding one that links not only storytellers and listeners but also books and readers.

I teach storytelling at the Graduate School of Library and Information Science at Dominican University in River Forest, Illinois. Most, although certainly not all, of my students plan to be youth services librarians in school or public libraries. This book is arranged along the lines of how I teach my class, starting with telling stories to preschoolers and moving toward adults, or, in this book's case, toward middle-schoolers ages 12 to 14 years old. To simplify the organization, this book is divided into the common age groupings often found in school or library storytelling events:

- 3 to 6 years old
- 6 to 9 years old
- 9 to 12 years old
- 12 to 14 years old

Depending on how your listening groups are arranged, you may often find yourself telling to groups organized a bit more broadly, and, in extreme situations, groups that include listeners from 3 to 14 years old. Luckily, developmental stages tend to be more tidal than concrete; that is, development tends to ebb and flow, with overlap occurring at all stages. Every child is an individual; each child is at a different place on the developmental path on any given day. Although we can't speak to specifics about each unique listener, we can speak to some observed generalities regarding group behavior.

Each chapter in this book builds on the previous chapter, introducing skills in small steps and expanding on them throughout the book. Every pertinent chapter includes very general characteristics of the ages being discussed, but please remember that the overlap among developmental stages is great; your own personal experiences with these various age groups will temper and inform the content of this book.

At the end of each chapter is a StoryCoaching entry, a retold folktale with instructions in italics as to how to most effectively tell the tale. Please remember that the StoryCoaching directions are suggestions, not rules, as every storyteller has his or her own individual style.

One reason we tell stories in classrooms and libraries is to promote the reading of books. Folktales, in single-tale volumes and collections, serve not only as sources for storytelling but also as resources for young readers. Each chapter in this book includes a Tales-to-Text list of suggested books for reading aloud or reading independently. Do not ignore the wealth of possibility already on your library shelves waiting to be shared through storytelling, reading aloud, or independent reading. The range of sophistication among picture book folktales makes some of them suitable for reading aloud to preschoolers and some suitable for reading alone by transitional, selective, and independent readers. The picture book is a format, not a genre; some picture books, such as Scott Cook's *The Gingerbread Boy*, attract very young listeners, while others, such as James Marshall's *Little Red Riding Hood*, interest transitional readers, and some, such as K. Y. Craft's *Cupid and Psyche*, appeal to as wide a range as 12 to 18 years old because of the sophistication of the art and the content.

Collections of folktales are sometimes organized thematically, and, depending on their layout and design, can appeal to sophisticated readers or motivate reluctant ones; consider, for example, Katrin Tchana's collection *The Serpent Slayer and Other Stories of Strong Women* or Matt Dembicki's graphic book *Trickster: Native American Tales, a Graphic Collection*. Adults often question the use of the picture book or graphic novel with independent readers; reassure them. The art and vocabulary in many folktale retellings are often sophisticated and challenging. Never underestimate the allure of effective illustration for the reluctant or selective reader, and never under-estimate the complexity of language in distinguished retellings of folktales, myths, and legends. While you are seeking tales to tell yourself, be aware of what you find that might entice the independent reader or the reader-aloud.

Chapters 2 through 5 end with four additional folktales for each specific age group retold specifically for this book. The folktales have been selected for retelling from public domain sources in order to avoid any copyright issues. The retelling of folktales face-to-face within a library or school setting is considered to be fair use under 17 U.S.C. Sect. 107. If the folktales are told as part of classroom instruction, there is additional protection under 17 U.S.C. Sect. 110(1). Shifting from live performance to recorded media (storytelling made available through podcast, video, or other online media) entails reproduction and distribution of copies of the works. In this case if the work is still under copyright, permission is generally needed.

All story and book recommendations have been used successfully with the designated ages and are widely available. For those who wish to investigate storytelling more extensively, many additional references are listed at the end of this book. None of the lists is comprehensive; rather, they include a selection of titles, classic and contemporary, that will guide you toward more in-depth information.

Folktales Aloud is not an academic approach to the history and place of storytelling in libraries; for that, see Greene and Del Negro's *Storytelling: Art and Technique*. This is not a book about connecting storytelling to pedagogy in the classroom; for that, see Norfolk, Stenson, and Williams's *The Storytelling Classroom: Applications across the Curriculum*. *Folktales Aloud* is an invitation to join a centuries-long celebration, where story is the guest of honor.

Welcome to the party.

Recommended Beginning Storytelling Books and Resources Mentioned

Cook, Scott. *The Gingerbread Boy*. Dragonfly, 1996.
Craft, K. Y. *Cupid and Psyche*. HarperCollins, 1996.

Dailey, Sheila. *Putting the World in a Nutshell: The Art of the Formula Tale.* H. W. Wilson, 1994.

Dembicki, Matt. *Trickster: Native American Tales, a Graphic Collection.* Fulcrum Books, 2010.

Galdone, Paul. *The Three Billy Goats Gruff.* Houghton, 1973.

Greene, Ellin. *Storytelling: Art and Technique.* With Janice M. Del Negro. Libraries Unlimited, 2010.

MacDonald, Margaret Read. *The Storyteller's Start-Up Book: Finding, Learning, Performing and Using Folktales.* August House, 2006.

———. *Twenty Tellable Tales: Audience Participation Folktales for the Beginning Storyteller.* American Library Association, 2004.

Marshall, James. *Little Red Riding Hood.* Dial, 1987.

Norfolk, Sherry, Jane Stenson, and Diane Williams. *The Storytelling Classroom: Applications across the Curriculum.* Libraries Unlimited, 2006.

Sawyer, Ruth. *The Way of the Storyteller.* Penguin, 1977.

Tchana, Katrin. *The Serpent Slayer and Other Stories of Strong Women.* Little, Brown, 2000.

Tolstoi, Aleksi. *The Great Big Enormous Turnip.* Illus. by Helen Oxenbury. Franklin Watts, 1969.

CHAPTER 2

STORYPLAY

Ages 3 to 6

Storyteller Frances Clarke Sayers once said that she knew exactly which of her brother's several girlfriends he should marry because this particular young woman told "The Gingerbread Boy" as if it were high tragedy ("From Me to You," in *Summoned by Books: Essays and Speeches*, Viking, 1965). This concept is important when telling stories to 3- to 6-year-olds: it is impossible to go over the top. The more you dramatize, the better children love it. Reach deep down inside, find your inner diva, and let her emote to the rafters.

Preschoolers and kindergartners learn through play. Learning through play is their natural state, and to work effectively with children this age storytellers have to remember, learn, or relearn what it means to play with story. To play means to surrender to the moment, to engage without self-consciousness, to be confident that the story will be enough. Playing with story is an effective way to spark young children's imaginations and expose them to new language and narrative structure. Playing with story is also a way to connect them—to you, to the library, and to each other—through a shared experience. Some professional storytellers will not work with preschoolers because they can't be controlled. I don't agree; preschoolers are unpredictable, not uncontrollable. If storytellers want a serene and orderly program, perhaps preschoolers are not their audience. This is not to say that a storyteller cannot successfully tell an oral story to this age group; it just has to be the right story. Preschoolers are more than ready to participate in a story; all they are waiting for is the storyteller's permission. To be successful with these children, a storyteller must be willing to invite and accompany the young listeners into storyplay, a realm these children can easily enter.

Librarians and teachers ready to try storytelling with preschoolers and kindergartners can add an oral story following the activities in a traditional storytime program. Two highly recommended resources to assist in planning are Judy Sierra's *Flannel Board Storytelling Book* (H. W. Wilson, 1987) and *Multicultural Folktales: Stories to Tell Young Children* (Oryx, 1996). These are triple-treat titles: varied story selections, simple patterns, and strong retellings that can be used even without the visual aid of the flannel board. These titles are older but still available, and there is nothing quite like them: the patterns are clean and easy to reproduce in various craft mediums, and the folktales themselves, retold by librarian, folklorist, author, and storyteller Sierra, need no adapting for successful telling.

When working with children in this age group, look for stories that have active plots with a strong forward momentum. Repetitive language such as refrains and rhymes appeal to the listening ear, as do songs and chants. Do not be concerned if you cannot carry a tune in a bucket; most of the children can't either. That doesn't stop them from singing—and it shouldn't stop you. Animal sounds are a winning element with this audience, so toss restraint to the wild winds and moo, meow, and roar until the room sounds like a menagerie. Stories wherein a small protagonist overcomes a large obstacle are favorites with this age as are tales with physical humor. Remember your audience here: to preschoolers physical humor includes things like sneezing, hiccupping, and snoring, all of which have great accompanying noises. Children ages 4 and 5 understand that stories have beginnings, middles, and endings. They can often retell at least parts of the story after hearing it, so encourage them to tell stories to their parents, caregivers, and siblings.

Any story you tell to these children should have a participatory element. At this age children are developing gross motor skills, and they often need some form of kinetic activity to keep them focused. Physical actions such as clapping, nodding, and making simple hand motions serve both as focus for and release of energy. Many of these children can skip or hop, and if they can't, they'll have fun trying.

Opportunities for verbal participation are easy to add. At 4 and 5 years old, most children are beginning to count to ten, so counting aloud is a good activity to add to many folktales. Any story with animals has the potential for an accumulation of animal sounds; any story with repetitive language has the potential for a preschool collective chorus. For example, the tale of "The Great Big Enormous Turnip" has opportunities for both choral repetition and animal noises. A farmer plants a turnip, and when he goes to pull it up, he discovers the turnip has grown so large he cannot get it out of the ground. He enlists the aid of his wife, their daughter, the horse, the cow, the dog, the cat, and finally the mouse. With the help of the littlest among them, the group manages to pull the reluctant root vegetable out of the ground. Various picture book versions of this tale are included at the end of this chapter. Preschoolers will easily join in on the repetitive language, appreciate the silliness of being unable to pull up a vegetable with the humorous name of *turnip*, and can usually make all of the required animal sounds, especially following an enthusiastic demonstration by the storyteller.

Children of this age enter into stories with abandon and enthusiasm. These young listeners enter into the story through the teller's invitation, metaphorically walking through the story hand-in-hand with the storyteller. The chronology of events is the path through the story. Know where the story begins, practice any repetitive refrains or noises, and know where the story ends. Keep to the narrative path of one thing after another, and you will successfully travel from the beginning to the end of the tale.

Folktales aimed at preschoolers and kindergartners work well because the structure, both narrative and linguistic, is so distinct. The most effective narrative form for an oral tale is simple and linear: a beginning, an initial problem or conflict, rising action, climax, and conclusion. Within that narrative form, language is key, and rhythmic, repetitive, and cumulative language works best with young children.

Preschoolers and kindergartners can follow simple directions, which makes acting out the story through creative dramatics a rewarding and fun storytelling activity. The trick is to get everyone involved. The children without specific parts might become a de facto Greek chorus, offering refrains, repetitive rhymes, accompanying noises, or commentary on the action of the story.

Take the folktale "The Three Billy Goats Gruff" for example, collected by Peter Christen Asbjørnsen and Jørgen Moe in the nineteenth century. Paul Galdone and Janet Stevens have both done picture book versions. If you are showing pictures as you tell the tale, Galdone's version is best; his palette may be acid green, but everyone will be able to see the images. If you are telling the story instead of reading it, however, it doesn't matter which book you use. Seeing the pictures is not an issue. Three billy goat brothers are longing to cross a bridge over a river to a field of fresh grass, but their way is blocked by the goat-gobbling troll who lives beneath the bridge. The two clever younger billy goats convince the troll to wait for their older brother, who is bigger and will make a more satisfying meal; the troll does so, to his regret, as the third billy goat brother tosses him into the river. Here is my simple adaptation of this old tale with instructions for telling. Please remember, these are suggestions, not rules.

STORYCOACHING

"The Three Billy Goats Gruff," adapted for telling by Janice M. Del Negro from
Popular Tales from the Norse **by Peter Christen Asbjørnsen and Jørgen Moe,**
trans. by George Webbe Dasent (Edmonston and Douglas, 1859).

Once upon a time there lived three billy goat brothers. Their name was Gruff, so they were called the Three Billy Goats Gruff.

Always make sure your listeners understand the basics of your tale. Ask very simple questions, provide very simple answers: "Do you know what a goat is? Have you seen goats at the zoo or on a farm? Do you know the kinds of sounds that billy goats make?" New vocabulary is not a problem; children will absorb new words and sounds easily, especially if they are repeated throughout the tale. The simple question also serves as an invitation to the listeners to participate in the telling of the tale.

Now these billy goat brothers liked nothing better than to eat, and they would eat just about anything, that being the nature of billy goats, but what they liked more than anything else in the world was to nibble nibble nibble on fresh green grass. And the freshest green grass was in the meadow that lay over the bridge that crossed the river.

This is a good place for repeating "nibble nibble nibble," adding in the goatly "baaaah!" and asking your listeners (if you have a lot of time) whether they like to nibble on grass, and if not, what their favorite thing to nibble on might be. Just a note: preschoolers love to talk about food. And pets. And just about anything else—they find the day-to-day fascinating, which is why simple stories like this one work so well with them.

The billy goat brothers wanted more than anything else to cross that bridge and eat the fresh green grass that grew on the other side, but there was a problem. To get to the meadow to eat the grass meant crossing the bridge, and crossing the bridge meant passing the troll that lived under the bridge. Now that troll was the meanest—well, think about the meanest person you know and this troll was meaner. Not only was he mean, he was hungry.

Ask children, "Do you get cranky when you get hungry?"

Well, this troll was so hungry he couldn't even remember when he hadn't been cranky. He just couldn't wait for something tasty to cross over his bridge, and he didn't have long to wait. Those billy goat brothers couldn't wait another minute to eat that fresh green grass, and the littlest Billy Goat Gruff plucked up his courage and started across the bridge. His sharp little hooves trippity-trapped on the bridge: Trippity-trap! Trippity-trap!

Clap your hands on your thighs or clap your hands together to imitate the "trippity-trap" sound; repeat the sound and motion several times with the children so they understand the routine and will feel free to join in when the sound/motion comes up again.

That trippity-trap wasn't very loud, but it was loud enough. Out from under the bridge came that wicked troll, and he roared, "Who's that going trippity-trap over my bridge?"

A word here about emoting with preschoolers and primary graders: it is almost impossible to go over the top with this age group. Think of storytelling to this age group as high melodrama; villains must twist their virtual moustaches and twirl their virtual capes. Think big, and then make it bigger.

The littlest Billy Goat Gruff stood firm in the middle of the bridge and said: "Maaaa! It is I, the littlest Billy Goat Gruff. I am going over the bridge, over the river, and into the meadow, to eat that fresh green grass and grow big and fat!"

The littlest billy goat can start with a small voice and a tiny bleat in a slightly higher pitch; the second and third billy goat brothers get physically larger and can have louder, lower-pitched bleats.

"Oh no you're not!" said the wicked troll. "You woke me up! Nobody wakes me up and lives to tell about it! I'm going to gobble gobble gobble you up!"

The troll is the villain and should be loud and growly, but not really scary. As much as preschoolers and primary graders say they want to be scared, they don't really mean it. They like the trappings of scary: the dark night, the full moon, the ghost that says "boo," but they don't really want to be really frightened.

"Oh don't gobble me up," said the littlest billy goat. "I am less than a measly mouthful! Wait for my brother, the second billy goat. He is bigger and tastier!"

And now a word on heroes: they are brave, bold, clever, and quick. Be confident in their presentation; they should be an obvious match for the villains.

"Bigger is better," said the hungry troll. "You go along and I will wait for the bigger billy goat brother!" So the littlest billy goat trippity-trapped over the bridge, over the river, and into the wide green meadow. There he rolled around in the fresh green grass and waited for his brothers.

Take advantage of the first billy goat's final actions to add a bleat and some yummy noises indicating the munching of grass.

It wasn't long before the second billy goat brother trippity-trippity-trapped across the bridge. Again that trippity-trap wasn't very loud, but it was loud enough. Out from under the bridge roared that wicked troll, "Who's that trippity-trapping over my bridge?"

Due to the increasing size of the billy goat brothers, the sound of the trippity-traps and bleating should become increasingly loud.

The second Billy Goat Gruff stood firm in the middle of the bridge and said, "It is I, the second Billy Goat Gruff. I am going over the bridge, over the river, and into the meadow to eat grass and grow big and fat!"

The second billy goat is louder and more substantive than the first.

"Oh no you're not!" said the wicked, hungry troll. "You woke me up! Nobody wakes me up and lives to tell about it! I'm going to gobble gobble gobble you up!"

Have fun with the troll roaring and the "gobble gobble gobble you up!" and your listeners will join right in.

"Oh don't gobble me up," said the second billy goat. "I am barely a measly mouthful! Wait for my brother, the third billy goat. He is much bigger and much tastier!"

"Bigger is better," said the hungry troll. "You go along and I will wait for the bigger billy goat brother!" So the second billy goat trippity-trapped, trippity-trapped over the bridge, over the river, and into the wide green meadow with the littlest billy goat. There they rolled around in the fresh green grass and waited for their brother.

Preschoolers will catch on to the repetition and predictability of the action; knowing that the two billy goat brothers are waiting for the third alleviates any real anxiety about his fate.

Before long the third billy goat brother trippity-trippity-trippity-trapped across the bridge. The third billy goat brother was so big that his trippity-trap sounded like thunder! Out from under the bridge roared that wicked troll, "Who's that trippity-trapping over my bridge?"

The big advantage to telling this story without the book is having the ability to look at your listeners and gauge their attention and response.

The third Billy Goat Gruff stood firm in the middle of the bridge and said, "It is I, the third Billy Goat Gruff. I am going over the bridge, over the river, and into the meadow, to eat grass and grow even bigger than I am already!"

The third billy goat is the biggest, loudest, and bravest; he is every bully's worst nightmare. Make him epic.

"Oh no you're not!" said the wicked, hungry troll. "You woke me up! Nobody wakes me up and lives to tell about it! I'm going to gobble gobble gobble you up!"

This is the climax of the tale. Take your time with the big billy goat's response to the troll; you have four lines to make this confrontation satisfying.

"Well, let's just see about that," said the third billy goat brother, and he pounded his hooves against the bridge and lowered his great curved horns. The troll came roaring out from under the bridge. "Maaaaa!" The third billy goat brother caught that troll in his great curved horns and tossed that troll over the side of the bridge and into the river with a great splash! "Maaaa!"

This is the defeat of the bully, the vanquishing of the villain; pause for a satisfying moment.

Then the third billy goat brother trippity-trippity-trippity-trapped over the bridge, over the river, into the green grassy meadow, and he and his brothers ate that fresh green grass, and if they haven't finished all that grass, well, they are eating it still! Trippity-trap, trippity-trap, trippity, trippity, trippity-trap!

Applaud your listeners and tell them what a fine job they did helping you tell the story.

Tales-to-Text

The titles listed here are not only resources for the storyteller but also suggested reading for children ages 3 to 6. The list includes picture book versions and variants of *The Three Billy Goats Gruff* and *The Enormous Turnip* along with other titles for storytelling and reading aloud. Additional suggestions can be found in the list of Folktale Picture Books in the References and Resources section.

Cousins, Lucy. *Yummy: Eight Favorite Fairy Tales.* Candlewick, 2009.

Davis, Aubrey. *The Enormous Potato*. Illus. by Dusan Petricic. Kids Can, 1999.

Dewan, Ted. *The Three Billy Goats Gruff*. Illus. by Ted Dean. Scholastic, 1995.

Emberley, Rebecca, and Ed Emberley. *Chicken Little*. Roaring Brook, 2009.

Emberley, Rebecca, and Ed Emberley. *The Red Hen*. Roaring Brook, 2010.

Galdone, Paul. *The Three Billy Goats Gruff*. Houghton, 1973.

Hester, Denia. *Grandma Lena's Big Ol' Turnip*. Illus. by Jackie Urbanovic. Albert Whitman, 2005.

Lum, Kate. *What! Cried Granny: An Almost Bedtime Story; A Silly, Funny Granny Tries to Put Her Grandson to Bed*. Penguin Putnam (Dial), 1999.

MacDonald, Margaret. *Go to Sleep, Gecko! A Balinese Folktale*. August House, 2006.

Ottolenghi, Carol. *The Three Billy Goats Gruff / Los Tres Chivitos*. Illus. by Mark Clapsadle. Keepsake, 2009.

Paye, Won-Ldy. *Mrs. Chicken and the Hungry Crocodile*. Henry Holt, 2003.

Peck, Jan. *The Giant Carrot*. Illus. by Barry Root. Dial, 1998.

Pinkney, Jerry. *The Lion and the Mouse*. Little, Brown Books for Young Readers, 2009.

Sierra, Judy. *Nursery Tales Around the World*. Illus. by Stefano Vitale. Clarion, 1996.

Stevens, Janet. *The Three Billy Goats Gruff*. Illus. by author. Sandpiper, 1995.

Tolstoy, Aleksei. *The Gigantic Turnip*. Illus. by Niamh Sharkey. Barefoot Books, 2009.

Zunshine, Tatiana. *A Little Story about a Big Turnip*. Illus. by Evgeny Antonenkov. Pumpkin House, 2004.

The Great Big Enormous Turnip

Ages 3–6. Retold by Janice M. Del Negro from *Russian Fairy Tales*, collected and edited by Alexander Afanasyev (K. Paul, 1864–1865).

This tale is playful and lighthearted, and what makes it a sure winner with children 3 to 6 years old is that it deals with two of their favorite things: animals and food. Tell this simple story like a tall tale, exaggerating the size of the turnip, the huffing and puffing and lack of success in pulling up the turnip, and the final triumphant harvesting. This cumulative tale can expand or contract by adding or subtracting characters to pull up the turnip. Don't forget the animal noises!

There was once a farmer who planted a garden, and in that garden he planted a turnip. (A turnip is a vegetable that grows underground, with only its leafy top sticking out.) Well, the turnip that the farmer planted? That turnip grew and grew and grew, until it was enormous! The leafy bits were almost as tall as a tree! The farmer grabbed hold of that turnip to pull that turnip out of the ground. He grabbed hold of those turnip leaves and he pulled and pulled and pulled—but nothing happened. So he did what he always did when things weren't working out—he called to his wife. Because on a farm, everybody helps.

The farmer's wife, she took hold of the farmer, the farmer grabbed hold of the turnip, and they pulled and they pulled and they pulled—but nothing happened. So the farmer's wife called her daughter. Because on a farm, everybody helps.

The daughter, she took hold of the farmer's wife, the farmer's wife, she took hold of the farmer, the farmer, he grabbed hold of the turnip, and they pulled and they pulled and they pulled—but nothing happened. So the daughter called the dog. Woof! Because on a farm, everybody helps.

The dog (woof!), he took hold of the daughter, the daughter, she took hold of the farmer's wife, the farmer's wife, she took hold of the farmer, the farmer, he grabbed hold of the turnip, and they pulled and they pulled and they pulled—but nothing happened. So the dog called the cat. Meow! Because on a farm, everybody helps.

The cat (meow!), she took hold of the dog, the dog (woof!), he took hold of the daughter, the daughter, she took hold of the farmer's wife, the farmer's wife, she took hold of the farmer, the farmer, he grabbed hold of the turnip, and they pulled and they pulled and they pulled—but nothing happened. So the cat called the mouse. Squeak! Because on a farm, everybody helps, even the littlest!

The mouse (squeak!), it took hold of the cat, the cat (meow!), she took hold of the dog, the dog (woof!), he took hold of the daughter, the daughter, she took hold of the farmer's wife, the farmer's wife, she took hold of the farmer, the farmer, he grabbed hold of the turnip, and they pulled and they pulled and they pulled . . . and they pulled and they pulled and they pulled . . .

and they pulled and they pulled and they pulled . . . and, finally! The turnip came up! Phew!

That turnip was so big the farmer and his wife invited all the neighbors over for dinner, and everybody—the farmer, the farmer's wife, their daughter, the dog (woof!), the cat (meow!), and the mouse (squeak!)—ate turnip stew, and turnip steak, and turnip pizza, and turnip ice cream, till they couldn't eat anymore. Because on a farm, everybody helps, and everybody eats, even the littlest!

The Hungry Wolf

Ages 3–6. Retold by Janice M. Del Negro from *More Russian Picture Tales* by Valerian Viliamovich Karrik (Frederick A. Stokes, 1914).

Stories with protagonists that outwit, outsmart, and outrun villains are big hits with listeners of all ages. In this tale a hapless (and hungry) wolf picks on the wrong animals for his dinner and suffers as a result. The cluelessness of the wolf combines with the attitudes of the disbelieving animals to make this a successful participation tale. Your listeners will be happy to howl! This is reminiscent of Patricia McKissack's Flossie and the Fox *(Dial, 1986), so don't forget those tales-to-text connections.*

There was once a wolf. He was big. He was hairy. He was hungry, so he went to see what he could find for dinner. After a bit the wolf saw a big-horned ram feeding in a meadow, and the wolf thought, "Ram stew! Yummy!"

The wolf went up to the ram and said, "Mr. Ram, Mr. Ram, I am going to eat you!"

But the ram looked over the wolf. "Who are you, I should like to know, that you think you are going to eat me?"

"I'm a wolf, and I'm looking for a good dinner," said the wolf.

"A wolf?" said the ram. "You're not a wolf, you're a dog. I don't mind being eaten by a wolf, but a dog? Never!"

"I am not a dog!" said the insulted wolf. "I'm a wolf. Aroooo!"

"Well, if you really are a wolf that's something else altogether," answered the ram. "If you really are a wolf, stand at the bottom of the hill and open your jaws wide. Then I'll run down the hill and jump straight into your mouth."

This sounded like a fine idea to the hungry wolf, so he raced to the bottom of the hill while the ram climbed to the top of the hill. The wolf opened his jaws wide. The ram ran down the hill as fast as he could and BAM! The ram hit the wolf with his big horns.

The wolf rolled over, knocked senseless with the blow, while the ram strolled along home. There lay the wolf, till at last he came to himself again, with all his bones aching.

"Well, what a fool I am!" thought the wolf. "Who ever saw a ram jump into a wolf's mouth of his own free will?"

The wolf was just as hungry as ever and wandered around looking for something without horns that he could eat. After a time he saw a horse in a meadow, nibbling the grass.

"Aha!" thought the wolf. "Horse steak!"

So the wolf went up to the horse and said, "Mr. Horse, Mr. Horse, I'm going to eat you!" But the horse answered, "Who are you, I should like to know, that you think you are going to eat me?"

"I'm a wolf, and I'm looking for a good dinner," said the wolf.

"A wolf?" said the horse. "Think again. You're not a wolf, you're a dog. I don't mind being eaten by a wolf, but a dog? Never!"

"I am not a dog!" shouted the insulted wolf. "I'm a wolf. Aroooo!"

"Oh, if you are sure you're a wolf, then it's all right," said the horse soothingly. "Only I'm not very fat yet, so you'd better start with my tail. Meanwhile I'll munch some more grass and get a little fatter."

This made sense to the wolf, so he went up to the horse from behind and was just going to take a big bite out of his tail, when the horse kicked the wolf with his back legs as hard as he could! BAM! The wolf rolled over, knocked out cold, while the horse galloped off.

There lay the wolf, till at last he came to himself again, with all his bones aching. The wolf thought, "Well, wasn't I a fool! Wasn't I a noodle! Who ever heard of anyone starting to eat a horse by the tail?"

The wolf was hungrier than ever and wandered around looking for something without strong back legs that he could eat. After a bit the wolf saw a pig rooting at the side of the road. The wolf looked at the pig carefully. No horns. And short legs. Finally! A possible dinner!

The wolf went up to the pig and said, "Mr. Pig, Mr. Pig, I'm going to eat you!"

But the pig answered, "Who are you, I should like to know, that you mean to eat me?"

"I'm a wolf, and I'm looking for a good dinner," said the wolf.

"A wolf?" said the pig. "Ha! I know a dog when I see one. I don't mind being eaten by a wolf, but a dog? Never!"

"I am not a dog!" shouted the insulted wolf. "I'm a wolf. Aroooo!"

"Oh, that's something else altogether then," answered the pig. "Well, you can't eat in the middle of the road. Climb on my back. I'll give you a ride to the woods, and then you can eat me."

"Oh, that is very kind of you," said the wolf, who really was exhausted after all his troubles. So he sat himself down on the pig's back, and the pig ran as fast as his little legs could carry him, straight into the center of the village.

"Wolf! Wolf!" cried the villagers, and all the dogs raced out from under porches, inside barns, and behind houses. Growling and snarling and showing their teeth, the dogs dashed for the wolf and chased him deep into the forest.

The hungry wolf never did get much dinner. Safe in the forest the wolf curled on top of a warm stone and howled gently at the rising moon. Aroooo!

The Teeny-Tiny Woman

Ages 3–6. Lightly retold by Janice M. Del Negro from *Popular Rhymes and Nursery Tales* by James Orchard Halliwell (John Russell Smith, 1849).

This is one of the simplest-to-tell tales for ages 3 to 6. The rhythmic language, refrains, and opportunities for participation are a clear invitation to the storytelling exchange between teller and listeners. This tale is the perfect go-to story when the really young ones want a scary story, because it has the trappings but is more funny than spooky. When you say the words "teeny-tiny" use a high-pitched, singsong voice that the children can imitate. When you reach the parts of the story where "teeny-tiny" is repeated in rapid succession, be ready for the giggles. The words "Give me my bone!" should be said in a low, deep voice to contrast with all those high-pitched "teeny-tiny"s. Success here depends on the modified jump-tale approach at the conclusion. A jump tale is a story in which the storyteller manipulates pace and volume in order to surprise listeners into an involuntary, collective response (see also the StoryCoaching story "Tailypo" in chapter 4).

Once upon a time there was a teeny-tiny woman who lived in a teeny-tiny house in a teeny-tiny town.

One day this teeny-tiny woman put on her teeny-tiny bonnet and went out of her teeny-tiny house to take a teeny-tiny walk. When this teeny-tiny woman had gone a teeny-tiny way, she came to a teeny-tiny gate. So the teeny-tiny woman opened the teeny-tiny gate—Squeak!—and went into a teeny-tiny graveyard. On a teeny-tiny grave she saw a teeny-tiny bone, and the teeny-tiny woman said to her teeny-tiny self, "This teeny-tiny bone will make me some teeny-tiny soup for my teeny-tiny supper."

So the teeny-tiny woman put the teeny-tiny bone into her teeny-tiny pocket and went home to her teeny-tiny house.

Now when the teeny-tiny woman got home to her teeny-tiny house, she was a teeny-tiny bit tired. So she went up her teeny-tiny stairs to her teeny-tiny bed and put the teeny-tiny bone into a teeny-tiny closet. When this teeny-tiny woman had been to sleep a teeny-tiny time, she was awakened by growly, whispery voice from the teeny-tiny closet, which said,

"Give me my bone!"

At this the teeny-tiny woman was a teeny-tiny bit frightened, so she hid her teeny-tiny head under the teeny-tiny blanket. When she had been hiding a teeny-tiny time, the growly, whispery voice again cried out from the teeny-tiny closet a teeny-tiny louder,

"Give me my bone!"

This made the teeny-tiny woman a teeny-tiny bit more frightened, so she hid her teeny-tiny head a teeny-tiny bit further under the teeny-tiny blanket. When the teeny-tiny woman had been hiding a teeny-tiny time, the growly, whispery voice from the teeny-tiny cupboard said again a teeny-tiny louder,

"Give me my bone!"

The teeny-tiny woman was a teeny-tiny bit more frightened, but she put her teeny-tiny head out of the teeny-tiny blanket, and said in her loudest teeny-tiny voice,

"TAKE IT!"

And the teeny-tiny woman took her teeny-tiny nap, and when she woke up she had a great big glass of milk and an even bigger cookie.

—— PLOP! Splash! A Folktale from Tibet ——

Ages 3–6. Retold by Janice M. Del Negro from sources including *Folk Tales from China* (Foreign Languages Press, 1959), *Tibetan Tales* by Anton Schiefner (Kegan Paul Trench Tübner, 1906), and *The Jataka, or, Stories of the Buddha's Former Births* by E. B. Cowell (Cambridge University Press, 1897).

This tale is reminiscent of "Henny-Penny" or "Chicken Little" in that pandemonium is caused by a mistake that is only discovered when some-one—in this case the snow leopard—refuses to panic. Different versions of this tale have a vast variety of animals; this retelling features animals that are indigenous to Tibet. Animal noises act as connecting tissue between the discrete events, so don't forget to roar, snort, and bellow with enthusiasm.

Long ago in the mountains of Tibet six rabbits lived on the shore of a lake. The lake was surrounded by bilva trees, covered with fine yellow fruit. One day, the biggest, ripest fruit on the biggest, tallest tree fell down into the lake. PLOP! Splash! The noise scared the rabbits so much, they took off running as fast as their legs could leap.

Racing underneath the trees the rabbits were spied by a monkey. "Where are you racing in such a hurry?" the monkey asked.

The rabbits said, "Can't stop! Can't stay! Plop is on the way!"

The monkey had never heard of a plop, but if it was enough to scare the rabbits, well, the monkey took off after them, swinging through the treetops.

The rabbits raced past a wild pig scavenging for roots. "Where are you racing in such a hurry?" the wild pig asked.

The rabbits said, "Can't stop! Can't stay! Plop is on the way!"

"Can't stay! Can't stop! Here comes plop!" cried the monkey.

The wild pig had never heard of a plop, but if it was enough to scare the rabbits, and the monkey too, well, the wild pig took off running after the rabbits.

On a small hill they passed a grazing gazelle. "Where are you racing in such a hurry?" the gazelle asked.

"Can't stop! Can't stay! Plop is on the way! Can't stay! Can't stop! Here comes plop!"

The gazelle had never heard of a plop before, but if it was enough to scare the rabbits, the monkey, and the wild pig too, well, the gazelle took off running on her long thin legs.

They passed a black bear munching on some nuts. "Where are you racing in such a hurry?" the bear asked.

"Can't stop! Can't stay! Plop is on the way! Can't stay! Can't stop! Here comes plop!" The bear had never heard of a plop before, but if it was enough to scare the rabbits, the monkey, the wild pig, and the gazelle too, well, the bear dropped the nuts and ran.

They passed a herd of wild yak with great curved horns munching tall grass. "Where are you racing in such a hurry?" a yak asked.

To the herd of wild yak all the animals cried: "Can't stop! Can't stay! Plop is on the way! Can't stay! Can't stop! Here comes plop!"

The herd of wild yak had never heard of a plop before, but if it was enough to scare the rabbits, the monkey, the wild pig, the gazelle, and the brown bear too, well, the yak lowered their great horns and the entire herd began to run. They ran and they ran.

The faster the animals ran the more frightened they became until they had no thought at all except to run faster and faster.

At the foot of the mountain a snow leopard lived in a cave of stone. When he caught sight of the yaks running, he roared to the largest of them all. "Brother! You have great horns and a thick coat, and you are the sturdiest of all the animals. Why are you running like mad?"

"Can't stop! Here comes plop!" cried the yak.

The snow leopard leapt and landed in front of the yak.

"Stop! What is a plop?" the snow leopard demanded.

The yak stopped.

"Well, I don't really know," the yak said.

"You don't know?" the snow leopard asked. "Why are you running from something when you don't even know what it is?"

"But the bear said . . ." the yak replied.

So the snow leopard asked the bear, who replied, "But the gazelle said . . ."

So the snow leopard asked the gazelle, who replied, "But the wild pig said . . ."

So the snow leopard asked the wild pig, who replied, "But the monkey said . . ."

So the snow leopard asked the monkey, who replied, "The rabbits! The rabbits were the first to warn about plop!"

The snow leopard went to the rabbits and patiently asked, "What is plop?"

"All six of us heard this terrible plop with our own ears," said the rabbits. "Come with us, and we'll show you where we heard it."

The rabbits led the snow leopard to the bilva trees on the edge of the lake, and pointing at the trees they told him, "The terrible plop is there."

Just then the biggest, ripest fruit on the biggest, tallest tree fell down into the lake. PLOP! Splash! The snow leopard laughed.

"That's it? You were running from a piece of fruit?" he said.

The animals felt a little silly. Someone called, "But the rabbits said . . ."

"Never mind what the rabbits said. Don't believe everything you hear. Plop! The sound of fruit dropping into the water is so terrifying? You almost ran your hearts out of your chests!"

The animals breathed a grateful sigh and threw themselves down to doze on the shore of the lake.

PLOP! Splash!

CHAPTER 3

COOPERATION AND COMMUNITY

Ages 6 to 9

Children ages 6 to 9 are usually enthusiastic about and receptive to storytelling. They participate, ask questions, and even tell their own stories. Structure in both story and program is as important to this age group as it is to preschoolers. The structure of the folktale is a built-in fail-safe for the audience and the teller.

Successful stories for preschoolers and primary graders have to consciously be chosen for elements that appeal to these young ages and levels of development: participation, repetition, humor. With younger listeners inexperienced storytellers sometimes err on the side of the too-sophisticated or abstract tale, because we storytellers tend to select those stories that we find appealing, and we are not preschoolers or primary graders. A conscious effort is required to recall the free-spirited enthusiasm younger listeners have for very simple tales. What we might consider repetitive and boring, they consider fun and reassuring.

Although some successful stories-for-telling will work with children ages 6 to 9 as well as younger children, older listeners are more socialized and are generally ready for slightly longer stories with more complex plots. Many children of this age are very literal, often friendly, and boisterously emotional. They like to play with language and are beginning to sequence events in chronological order. They can identify characters in stories and differentiate between reality (what really happens day-to-day) and fantasy (talking animals that act like people). Still, some of the same advice for telling to younger children applies to this age group: use drama at an operatic scale, maintain a high energy level, and select participation stories whenever possible.

A common impulse among those who tell stories to preschool listeners is to introduce the standard canon of European folktales—"Sleeping Beauty," "Snow White," or "Hansel and Gretel." This approach doesn't always work. These stories can be told to younger listeners, but many of the versions available are overly descriptive and too conceptually advanced for young children; they do not lend themselves to telling aloud without extensive adaptation. (Try reading Trina Schart Hyman's *Little Red Riding Hood* aloud to a group of preschoolers and see how many minutes it actually takes.) Children ages 6 to 9, on the other hand, are a receptive audience for these tales. Even so, tales must be chosen carefully, as some popular anthologized or picture book versions tend to be overwritten. James Marshall's retold and illustrated picture book folktales are stellar exceptions. Traditional tales with moral lessons (inherent, not pedantic), such as Paul Galdone's *The Magic Porridge Pot* or variants of "Stone Soup," work well with this age group, as do fables from Aesop and La Fontaine.

This audience is still interested in audience participation stories and songs and will willingly participate in circle games and creative dramatics. Six-year-olds are better at following directions than 3-year-olds, and this ability improves as they get older. Although they may be able to sit quietly for longer periods of time than preschoolers, it is still a very good idea to build participation and some physical activity into any storytelling experience for these listeners.

It is easy to be the librarian or teacher for the child who takes to reading effortlessly; this child is easy to accommodate and direct. The child who does not take to reading quite so easily needs exposure to language and narrative structure in ways other than through text. Storytelling is the perfect alternative activity because it works with children at all literacy levels.

Children 6 to 9 years old are acquiring the skills that will make them better readers. As librarians and teachers know, some children come to school unprepared, without the vocabularies children their age need to facilitate their literacy and literary journeys. Storytelling exposes children to language in a playful way, increasing children's vocabularies as they listen and as they participate in the tales. Retelling stories helps enrich children's vocabulary and adds knowledge of story structure, making narrative elements recognizable when children meet them in written texts. Listening, telling, and retelling are playfully purposeful activities that not only help create community in the library and in the classroom but also assist in the acquisition of vital literacy skills (see Greene and Del Negro, *Storytelling: Art and Technique*, and MacDonald, *Twenty Tellable Tales: Audience Participation Folktales for the Beginning Storyteller*).

Children's ability to actively participate in story creation increases once they begin to master basic reading skills. Think of reader's theater as a text-based offshoot of storytelling. The storyteller (or the group) adapts a story into a formal script; then reader's theater participants read the story aloud using the script. Aaron Shepard's excellent website (www.aaronshep.com) has already-developed scripts as well as guides to developing your own reader's theater folktale scripts. Scriptwriting can be specifically tailored to group members, who can be introduced to the story through listening first and then, if possible, through reading. This activity is a boon for the reluctant or nervous reader-aloud, since it allows practice before reading and does not demand a cold reading in front of a group.

Children 6 to 9 years of age are the perfect troupe for creative dramatics, defined for the purposes of this text as acting out a heard story. In contrast to younger listeners, those 6 to 9 years old have the language and physical capabilities necessary to make them active participants in story creation. The advantage of storytelling and creative dramatics is that these activities include everyone; even the child who is not a reader can participate in retelling or acting out a heard story. The process of moving a story from telling to creative dramatics allows participation on many levels. A storyteller can tell the story to the group and then have the group tell the story back to the teller in a type of call-and-response activity. Children can volunteer or be chosen to play a particular part, and the story can be acted out right on the spot. Remember, this is not a test; any time the story players get stuck, the storyteller—or the group—provides the answers and suggestions that move the story forward. Although the storyteller still needs to direct, children of this age can take over not only character roles in the story but narrative roles as well; some are even enthusiastic and creative improvisers.

Ideally, the worldview of children this age is expanding, which makes this a good time to introduce international folktales, such as Jataka tales from India and world folktales retold by Virginia Haviland. "Tipingee," in Diane Wolkstein's collection of tales from Haiti titled *The Magic Orange Tree and other Haitian Folktales*, or "Why Frog and Snake Never Play Together" from *Ashley Bryan's African Tales, Uh-Huh* also move smoothly from the written to the spoken word. Always have the book on hand to make the connection between the story and the text from which it comes.

Children ages 6 to 9 tend to enjoy stories with action and humor that have motivations, emotions, and characters to which they can relate. European canonical folktales, such as "Jack and the Beanstalk," selected tales from the Brothers Grimm, humorous Jack Tales from the American Appalachians, and how-and-why stories from a wide variety of world cultures appeal to these listeners. The humorous scary tale also works well with this age group (in fact the scary story wins with listeners of all ages), so brush off the suspenseful and well-paced "Hansel and Gretel" for an introduction to a classic folktale.

The length of stories for this age group can be anywhere from five to twenty minutes, depending on how familiar the group is with listening to stories; more experienced listeners tend to be able to listen to longer tales. To capture this age group, storytellers must be able to hold their listeners, which means being very aware of the high and low points of interest in the tale and adjusting the telling speed or pace accordingly. For example, dialogue tends to make a story lively, while straight narrative can be less engaging. A longer story requires more dialogue to break up the narrative and a quicker pace in parts of the story that are mostly description. What about stories that don't use dialogue? Simple—add it. Instead of narrating a descriptive passage, have a character speak to supply the necessary information.

A tremendous variety of folktales works for children in this age group, including fables and humorous ghost-and-gore stories. Many cultures have a wide range of teaching tales, or fables; the most well-known in the United States are the fables of Aesop. Using fables can be tricky, because fables as offered in most anthologies are very short and have little arc; that is, they lack momentum and tension, basic elements of a well-told tale. Aesop's fables and those written by La Fontaine lend themselves to storytelling if the teller is willing to expand on the existing text by including dialogue exchanges or even contemporary references. Good examples of playing with fables are Jane Yolen's *A Sip of Aesop* and Brad Sneed's *Aesop's Fables.*

Jean de La Fontaine wrote many original fables, but he also sometimes retold selected Aesop's fables, which is why you may find the same fables in collections by each author. More often than not fables need a little retelling to give them a heightened sense of drama. Consider the tale of the battle between the North Wind and the Sun, which can be found in both La Fontaine and Aesop. Summarized, Wind and Sun are arguing as to who is stronger when they spy a traveler on the road. They decide that the one who can make the traveler take off his coat is the stronger. The Wind goes first. He blows and blows, but only succeeds in making the traveler pull his coat closer around himself. When the Sun takes his turn, he covers the traveler with warm rays, and the man removes his coat. The moral of the story is clear and pertinent to young listeners: gentle warmth can accomplish what forceful bullying cannot. There are many versions of this tale. One particularly good version is *The North Wind and the Sun*, illustrated by Brian Wildsmith. Another is Heather Forest's retelling, *The Contest between the Sun and the Wind.* This particular tale is fun to tell and retell, with opportunities for some over-the-top characterizations and physicality. The story is straightforward but powerful. It is simple enough for primary graders to retell easily, and its moral or message will resonate long after the fact.

STORYCOACHING

"The North Wind and the Sun," retold by Janice M. Del Negro; versions available by La Fontaine and Aesop.

Up in the clear blue sky the cold North Wind blew around the warm, glowing Sun.

Opening moments are crucial. A quiet pause and an outstretched hand both indicate "now we begin." Opening sentences must be deliberate and emphatic; do not throw away the moment—make it count. Traditional language, such as "once upon a time" or "long ago and far away," is a cue to the listening audience that the story has begun.

"I am much stronger than you are, Sun," the North Wind said. "I make kites fly, boats sink, and leaves fall."

The North Wind is a boastful sort, so he needs a voice and a demeanor that express his overblown character. An increase in volume and a posture that indicates excessive pride work here. Audience participation can be invited by adding a "whoosh!" noise, or by puffing out your cheeks to blow big breaths, or by doing both.

"You are strong, anyone can see," said the Sun. "But I am strong too. I make flowers bloom, and wheat grow, and . . ."

The Sun is fair and smart, so the storyteller's voice should reflect that fairness. Tone of voice should be warm and reasonable.

"Oh, that is nothing," said the Wind. "That is just heat. I can blow ships across the sea and clouds across the sky. Why, there is nothing I cannot move with my great gusts!"

The Wind gets even more obnoxious here, laughing and boastful, voice big and booming. Tell the children to puff out their cheeks and blow like the wind! Make sure you demonstrate enthusiastically.

The Wind blew a cloud right into the Sun's shining face. Now the Sun was a little irritated.

Wave away the cloud in the Sun's face. Big gestures and a little cough indicate the Sun's displeasure.

"Do you want to bet?" said the Sun.

Now the Sun is angry, so the Sun's voice must reflect that anger and irritation. Here is a good spot to fall into colloquial language—"do you wanna bet?" Think of it as siblings arguing over a toy.

The North Wind howled with laughter.

Ask your listeners: How do you think the wind would sound if it were laughing?

"Oh, I am sure to win that bet!"

The Wind is a big, blustery bully. He should be loud and obnoxious.

"Really?" asked the Sun. "I wouldn't be so sure."

The Sun is brave, and irritated, and willing to take on this bully.

"Oh, I am sure!" howled the Wind.
"Alright, then," said the Sun. "What shall we bet?"

A short lesson on story geography: when two characters are speaking to one another, the storyteller must indicate by body language and eye contact the location of each speaker in order to make it clear to listeners which character is speaking at any given moment. For example, if the Wind speaks from the left, he must always speak from the left; a slight turn of the body or head can indicate this. The same goes for the Sun: if the Wind speaks from the left and the Sun speaks from the right, they must always speak from those locations. Characters—and narrator—should almost always speak to the listeners; eye contact between storyteller and listeners is a key element in maintaining attention and concentration. Sometimes, though, it is worthwhile (for a laugh or for emphasis) to have one character speak directly to the other. Establishing the geography of the story—that is, where each character is physically located—will help storyteller and listeners keep a clear picture of the action in their minds.

"Let's see," said the Wind, and he gazed down at the green earth. There, far below on a narrow country road, walked a traveler in a long woolen cloak.

Look down at the ground briefly, as if you are the Wind looking at the traveler; point to the man on the road and look back at your listeners.

"Do you see that traveler there? Whoever can get the traveler to take off his cloak will be the winner."

"Alright then," said the Sun. "You first."

Think about whether the Sun knows he can win this bet. If he knows he can win, how will he sound?

"Oh ho!" laughed the Wind. "Now you will see how strong I really am! I will blow that cloak right off his shoulder!"

Whoosh noises.

The North Wind began to blow.

Whoosh noises.

The sky turned gray and cloudy. The Wind blew fiercely into the traveler's face, blowing around his ears and sending his hat flying.

Point to the hat flying away.

The traveler scurried after his hat and jammed it farther down on his head to cover his ears.

Hold your fists beside your ears to indicate the traveler hanging on to his hat.

The Wind blew wildly at the traveler's legs, blowing the cloak out behind the traveler. The traveler grabbed the edges of his cloak and pulled it tight across his chest and up under his chin.

Wrap your arms around your upper body to mimic the traveler holding his cloak.

The Wind blew so hard, he blew the birds right out of the sky.

Look up at the birds; follow them with your eyes or head or both as they fall to the ground.

The Wind blew so hard the traveler could barely walk.

Whoosh!

The Wind blew so hard the traveler felt winter had come again.

Whoosh!

The Wind blew so hard the traveler held his cloak as tight as he could.

Whoosh!

The traveler clutched his cloak, held on to his hat, and leaned into the Wind, trying to walk against the gale. The Wind blew and blew and blew, and the traveler held his cloak. The more the Wind blew, the more tightly the traveler held his cloak. After a long while, even the Wind ran out of breath.

Each time the Wind blows, puff out your cheeks and blow vociferously; when the Wind runs out of breath, the storyteller should, too.

"I don't understand it," the Wind gasped. "I blew as hard as I could."

The Wind is gasping for air at this point, huffing and puffing and out of breath. Encourage the children to huff and puff along with you.

"Let me try," said the Sun.
The Sun looked down at the freezing traveler and smiled.

Look down on your listeners and smile.

The Sun's smile was warm. The Sun's smile was cheery.

Hold out your arms as if they are the rays of the Sun.

The sky turned bright, and the birds crept out of their trees and began to sing.

Add a few tweet-tweets here and encourage listener tweeting.

The traveler loosed his cloak from around his throat, and the Sun shone upon him.

The storyteller's voice should be warm and calm, friendly and inviting.

The Sun glowed golden and friendly in the bright blue sky. The traveler took off his hat and pulled his handkerchief out of his pocket to wipe his forehead.

Wipe your forehead with the back of your hand; don't be surprised if the children do, too.

The Sun danced warmly around the traveler.

Hold out your arms and beam.

The traveler pushed back his hat. The Sun beamed happy beams.

Hold out your arms and beam; wiggle your fingers to indicate dancing sunbeams.

The traveler took off his hat. He took off his cloak. He came to a river, and he was so warm he took off all his clothes and jumped in! Splash!

Clap your hands and then spread them up and apart to indicate the size of the splash.

The Sun sparkled on the water, and the North Wind had to admit the Sun was indeed stronger. The winner! Hooray!

Hold up your hands clasped together in the winner gesture. Invite listeners to cheer the Sun and themselves.

Tales-to-Text

Aesop. *Aesop's Fables*. Retold and illus. by Jerry Pinkney. SeaStar Books, 2000.

———. *Aesop's Fables*. Retold and illus. by Brad Sneed. Dial, 2003.

———. *The Boy Who Cried Wolf*. Retold by B. G. Hennessy. Simon and Schuster, 2006.

————. *The Lion and the Mouse*. Retold and illus. by Jerry Pinkney. Little, Brown, 2009.

Birdseye, Tom, adapter. *Soap! Soap! Soap! Don't Forget the Soap! An Appalachian Folktale*. Illus. by Andrew Glass. Holiday House, 1993.

Brown, Marcia. *Stone Soup*. Scribner, 1947.

Bryan, Ashley. *Ashley Bryan's African Tales, Uh-Huh*. Atheneum, 1998.

Claflin, Willy. *The Uglified Ducky*. August House, 2008.

Codell, Esmé Raji. *Fairly Fairy Tales*. Illus. by Elisa Chavarri. Aladdin, 2011.

Demi. *Buddha Stories*. Henry Holt, 1997.

Forest, Heather. *The Contest between the Sun and the Wind*. August House, 2007.

Galdone, Paul. *The Magic Porridge Pot*. Clarion, 1979.

Gibb, Sarah. *Rapunzel*. Albert Whitman, 2011.

Grimm Brothers. *About Wise Men and Simpletons*. Trans. by Elizabeth Shub. Etchings by Nonny Hogrogian. MacMillan, 1971.

————. *More Tales from Grimm*. Freely translated and illustrated by Wanda Gág. University of Minnesota Press, 2006.

————. *Tales from Grimm*. Freely translated and illustrated by Wanda Gág. University of Minnesota Press, 2006.

Haviland, Virginia. *Favorite Fairy Tales Told Around the World*. Illus. by S. D. Schindler. Little, Brown, 1985.

Hawes, Alison. *The Wind and the Sun*. Illus. by Bee Willey. Rigby Educational Publishers, 2007.

Hayes, Joe. *The Day It Snowed Tortillas/El Día que Nevaron Tortillas*. Cinco Puntos Press, 2003.

Hoberman, Mary Ann. *Very Short Fables to Read Together*. Illus. by Michael Emberley. Little, Brown, 2010.

Hoena, Blake A. *Jack and the Beanstalk: The Graphic Novel*. Stone Arch Books, 2009.

La Fontaine, Jean de. *The Hare and the Tortoise and Other Fables of La Fontaine*. Illus. by Giselle Potter. Barefoot Books, 2006.

———. *The North Wind and the Sun: A Fable*. Illus. by Brian Wildsmith. Franklin Watts, 1964.

Lee, Jeanne M. *I Once Was a Monkey: Stories Buddha Told*. Farrar, Straus and Giroux, 1999.

Lowry, Amy. *Fox Tails: Four Fables from Aesop*. Holiday House, 2012.

McGovern, Ann. *Stone Soup*. Illus. by Winslow Pinney Pels. Scholastic, 1986.

Muth, Jon J. *Stone Soup*. Illus. by the author. Scholastic, 2003.

O'Malley, Kevin. *The Great Race*. Walker, 2011.

Palatini, Margie. *Lousy Rotten Stinkin' Grapes*. Illus. by Barry Moser. Simon and Schuster, 2009.

Sierra, Judy. *Wiley and the Hairy Man*. Illus. by Brian Pinkney. Lodestar Books, 1996.

Stanley, Diane. *The Giant and the Beanstalk*. HarperCollins, 2004.

Walker, Richard. Jack and the Beanstalk. Illus. by Niamh Sharkey. Barefoot Books, 2006.

Ward, Helen. *Unwitting Wisdom: An Anthology of Aesop's Fables*. Chronicle Books, 2004.

Washington, Donna. *Big Scary House*. Illus. by Jacqueline Rogers. Hyperion/Jump at the Sun, 2000.

Wolkstein, Diane. *The Magic Orange Tree and Other Haitian Folktales*. Schocken Books, 1987.

Yolen, Jane. *A Sip of Aesop*. Illus. by Karen Barbour. Blue Sky, 1995.

The Hedley Kow

Ages 6–9. Retold by Janice M. Del Negro from *More English Fairy Tales*
by Joseph Jacobs (David Nutt, 1890).

*Introduce this story by explaining that Hedley is a village in England and
that the kow (sometimes pronounced like the coo of a dove) is a shape-
changing creature that likes to make mischief. The merry old woman is
a happy old soul, so her cheerfulness should be evident throughout.*

Once there was a merry old woman who lived in the village of
Hedley. Hedley was a cheery old town in the daylight, but at
night Hedley was not so cheery. At night Hedley was haunted by a
bogle, a shape-shifting creature called the Hedley Kow. The Hedley
Kow made larky mischief of one kind and another, from mooing
into a cow who tipped over the milk bucket to buzzing into a mos-
quito who bit the dog's ear. All the villagers had stories about the
Hedley Kow, but the merry old woman had none.

Now the merry old woman earned her way in the world by
doing this and that for the farmers' wives who lived in Hedley. She
rocked babies, baked bread, and even sheared the occasional sheep.
The merry old woman earned a penny here and a potato there, and

with bread and butter at one house and a cup of tea at another, she made do.

Well, one summer evening she finished up her chores and was trotting away home with a payment of carrots and onions, when what should she see but a big black pot with a big black lid sitting right in the middle of the road.

The merry old woman stopped. "Bless my buttons! Aren't I the luckiest soul in the wide rosy world? This is just the very thing for my carrots and onions! But who can have left it here?" She looked all round for the person the pot belonged to, but the merry old woman was all alone.

"Maybe it has a hole in the bottom," said the merry old woman, "and that's why someone left it in the middle of the road. But wouldn't that be lucky? I can put flowers in it and sit it in the window! I'll just take it home with me, hole in the bottom or not." And she lifted the lid to look inside.

But when she looked inside, do you think she saw a hole in the bottom of the pot? No!

"Bless my buttons! Aren't I the luckiest soul in the wide rosy world?" she cried. "This pot is full to the very top with gold coins!"

For a while the merry old woman walked round and round the big black pot, admiring the glittery gold and saying, "Well, bless my buttons! I do feel rich and grand!" But the sun was going down, and the merry old woman needed to go home, so she fastened one end of her shawl to the pot—for it was heavy with gold—and dragged it along behind her.

"I could buy a grand house and live like a queen, and do nothing all day but sit by the fire with a cup of tea! Or maybe I'll just bury it in a hole at the end of the garden. Or maybe I'll decorate the chimney with it, or . . . oh, I feel so grand, I don't know myself at all!"

By this time the merry old woman was a bit tired of dragging that big black pot of glittery gold—gold is very heavy, you know—so she stopped to rest for a minute, looking to see that her treasure was safe.

But when she looked she saw the big black pot wasn't full of glittery gold at all, but sparkly silver coins instead.

She stared at it, and rubbed her eyes and stared at it again, but she couldn't make it look like anything but sparkly silver coins. "Well, bless my buttons!" she said. "Aren't I the luckiest soul in the wide rosy world?" she cried. "Silver is so much easier to look after than gold. Gold coins would be such a bother—sparkly silver is far less trouble and more than I'll ever need."

So the merry old woman set off home again, cheerfully planning all the grand things she was going to do with her money. It wasn't very long, however, before she got tired again and stopped to rest for a minute or two, looking to see that her treasure was safe.

But when she looked she saw the big black pot wasn't full of silver at all. It wasn't even a pot at all, but a great big lump of iron instead!

She stared at it, and rubbed her eyes and stared at it again, but she couldn't make it look like anything but a great big lump of iron. "Well, bless my buttons!" she said. "Aren't I the luckiest soul in the wide rosy world?" she cried. "Now it's a great big lump of iron! Well, that is just so handy! I can sell that iron, easy-peasy, and get a lot of copper pennies for it. Oh, it's so much better than gold or silver, and iron will sell for more copper pennies than I can spend. Rich? I'll just be rolling!"

The merry old woman trotted on chuckling at her good luck, till presently she glanced over her shoulder.

"Well, bless my buttons! Aren't I the luckiest soul in the wide rosy world?" she cried. "That great big lump of iron has turned itself into a great big stone! Now, how could it have known I needed something to hold open my front door? Oh, it's a fine thing to have such good luck!"

All in a hurry to see how the stone would look holding open her door, she trotted down the hill and stopped at the bottom beside her own little gate.

The merry old woman unlatched the gate, and she turned to pick up the stone. The stone lay still as, well, a stone on the grassy path. There was plenty of light, and the merry old woman could see plain as plain as she picked up the stone.

All of a sudden, the stone jumped right out of her hands, spun around in the air, and grew in a moment as big as a horse! In front of the merry old woman's wide surprised eyes, the stone grew four lanky legs, a horse's head, two long ears, and a spindly tail. With a wild whinny the creature kicked its feet into the air and ran off whinny-ninny into the woods!

The merry old woman stared after it, till it was fairly out of sight.

"Well, bless my buttons," she said at last. "If that was not the Hedley Kow I don't know my own name! I am the luckiest soul in the wide rosy world! Fancy me seeing the Hedley Kow all to myself! I can tell you, I *do* feel that GRAND!"

So the merry old woman went into her cottage and sat down by the fire to chuckle over her good luck.

She didn't have gold and she didn't have silver, she didn't have iron and she didn't have copper, but she did have a story to last her whole life long, and that made her feel GRAND!

—————— Jack and His Comrades ——————

Ages 6–9. This is a variant of "The Bremen Town Musicians," retold by Janice M. Del Negro from multiple sources, including Patrick Kennedy's *Legendary Fictions of the Irish Celts* (Macmillan, 1866), Francis L. Palmer's version from his Chicopee, Massachusetts, grandfather for the *American Folk-Lore Journal* (vol. 1, 1888), and Fannie D. Bergen's version as told in Mansfield, Ohio, for the *American Folk-Lore Journal* (vol. 1, 1888). For those interested in how stories travel, there is another version of this tale entitled "The World's Reward" in *South-African Folk-Tales* by James A. Honeÿ (Baker and Taylor, 1910) as well as a version in *Jack Tales* by Richard Chase (Houghton Mifflin, 2003).

When telling this tale emphasize Jack's optimistic good nature and his sense of humor; after all, it isn't everybody who can talk to unfortunate (but optimistic) beasts. Insert the occasional animal sound for comic relief.

Once there was a poor widow who had one son named Jack. Times were very hard, and Jack and his mother didn't know how they'd

live till the new potatoes would be fit for eating. So Jack said to
his mother one evening, "Mother, bake my bread and kill my hen.
I'll go seek my fortune, and if I meet it, never fear but I'll soon be
back to share it with you."

So Jack's mother did as he asked her. She used the last of the
flour to bake him some bread, killed and cooked the scrawny
chicken, and packed them up for her son's journey. He set out
at break of day, and his mother came along with him to the yard
gate.

"Jack," she says, says she, "which would you rather have, half
the bread and half the hen with my blessing, or the whole of them
both with my curse?"

"O mother mine," says Jack, says he, "You know I wouldn't
have your curse if all the world's riches went along with it."

"Well, then, Jack," says she, "here's the whole loaf of bread and
the whole roasted chicken with my thousand blessings along with
them." So Jack's mother stood at the gate and blessed him as far as
her eyes could see him.

Well, he went along and he went along asking at every farm
along the way for work, till he had sore feet and a sorry heart and
not one job to show for it. At last his road led by the side of a
swamp, and there was a poor donkey up to his shoulders in the
muck.

"Ah, Jack," the donkey says, "help me out or I'll be drowned."

"Don't ask me twice," says Jack, and he pitched big stones and
sods into the muck, till the donkey was able to climb out.

"Thank you, Jack," says the donkey, when he was out on the hard road. "I'll do as much for you some time. Where are you going?"

"I'm going to seek my fortune if luck will have it!" said Jack.

"I'll go along with you," says the donkey. "Maybe we'll have better luck together."

"Bless my soul, perhaps we will," says Jack, and down the road they went.

Well, they were going through a village, where a whole army of barefoot boys were chasing a poor dog with cans tied to his tail. The dog ran up to Jack for protection, and the donkey let out such a roar that those beastly boys took to their heels as if the devil was after them.

"More power to you, Jack," says the dog. "I am much obliged. Where are you going?"

"We're going to seek our fortunes if luck will have it!" said Jack.

"I'd be proud to go with you!" says the dog. "Maybe we'll have better luck together."

"Bless my soul, perhaps we will," says Jack. "Throw your tail over your arm and come along."

They got outside the town and sat down under an old wall, and Jack pulled out his bread and meat and shared with the dog, and the donkey made his dinner on a bunch of thistles. While they were eating and chatting, what should come by but a poor half-starved cat, and the meorow she gave out would make a stone heart ache.

"You poor puss," says Jack. "Here's a bone and something on it."

"May your child never know a hungry belly!" says the cat. "Thank you for your kindness. May I be so bold as to ask where you are all going?"

"We're going to seek our fortunes if luck will have it!" said Jack.

"I'd be proud to go with you!" says the cat. "Maybe we'll have better luck together."

"Bless my soul, perhaps we will," says Jack. "The more the merrier, I say."

Off they set again, and just as the shadows of the trees were three times as long as themselves, they heard a great cackling in a field beside the road, and out over the ditch jumped a fox with a fine black rooster in his mouth.

"Oh, you villain!" says the donkey, roaring like thunder.

"At him, good dog!" says Jack, and the words weren't out of his mouth when the dog took off after the fox, who dropped that rooster and was off like a shot. The poor rooster came fluttering and trembling to Jack and his comrades.

"O kindest of neighbors!" says the rooster, "wasn't it the best of luck that threw you in my way? I will remember your kindness if ever you find hardship, and where in the world are you all going?"

"We're going to seek our fortunes if luck will have it," said Jack.

"I'd be proud to go with you!" says the rooster. "Maybe we'll have better luck together."

"Bless my soul, perhaps we will," says Jack. "The more the merrier!"

Well, the march began again, and just as the sun was gone down they looked around, and there was neither cabin nor farmhouse in sight.

"Well, well," says Jack, "the worse luck now the better another time, and it's only a summer night after all. We'll go into the wood, and make our bed in the grass."

No sooner said than done. Jack stretched himself down on a bunch of dry grass, the donkey lay near him, the dog and cat lay in the donkey's warm lap, and the rooster went to roost in the closest tree.

Well, the soundness of deep sleep was over them all, when the rooster began to crow.

"Bother, you silly rooster!" says the donkey. "You woke us all! What's the matter?"

"It's daybreak, that's the matter. Don't you see light yonder?"

"I see a light," says Jack, "but it's from a candle, not the sun. Now that we're awake we may as well go over and ask for a real bed."

So they all shook themselves awake and went on through grass and rocks and hillocks till they got down into a hollow, and there was the light coming through the shadow, and along with it came loud singing and louder laughing and even louder shouting.

"Easy, now!" says Jack. "Walk on your tippy-toes till we see what sort of people we have to deal with here."

So they crept near the window, and there they saw six robbers inside, with pistols and cutlasses, sitting at a table, eating roast beef and pork, and drinking mulled punch and cider.

"Wasn't that a fine haul we made!" says one ugly-looking thief with his mouth full. "We have enough to last a good long while! Here's to stealing and cheating!"

"To stealing and cheating!" cried out every one of those bad men, and Jack put his finger over his lips.

"Shhhhh! Come close, my friends," says he in a whisper, and he told them his plan.

The donkey put his fore-hooves on the window sill, the dog got on the donkey's head, the cat on the dog's head, and the rooster on the cat's head. Then Jack made a sign, and they all sang out like mad.

"Hee-haw, hee-haw!" roared the donkey; "bow-wow!" barked the dog; "meorow-meorow!" cried the cat; "cock-a-doodle-doo!" crowed the rooster.

"Level your pistols!" shouted Jack, "and make smithereens of 'em. Don't leave a mother's son of 'em alive; ready, aim, fire!"

With that the animals gave a great roar and smashed every pane in the window. Glass flew everywhere. The robbers were frightened out of their wits! They blew out the candles, threw down the table, and skelped out at the back door, and never stopped running till they were in the very heart of the wood.

Jack and his friends laughed so hard they almost cried. They got into the cabin, closed the shutters, lit the candles, and ate and drank till they couldn't eat or drink anymore. Then they lay down to rest, Jack in the bed, the donkey in the yard, the dog on the doormat, the cat by the fire, and the rooster on the ledge above the front door.

At first the robbers were very glad to find themselves safe in the thick wood, but then . . .

"All the gold and silver that we left behind!" moaned those crooks.

"I think I'll venture back," says the captain crook, "and see if we can get our treasure."

"That's a good man!" says all, when of course he wasn't, but away he went anyway.

The lights were all out, and so the captain crook groped his way inside. He went to the fireplace and tried to light a match on a burning red coal, except it wasn't a coal at all, but the eye of the cat glowing in the dark. The cat gave a great hiss and flew at the thief, and tore him with teeth and claws. The thief gave out a roar and started across the room, but he trod on the dog's tail, and the dog put the marks of his teeth in that crook's arms and legs.

"A thousand murders!" cried the crook. "I wish I was out of this cursed house!"

When the crook got to the door, the rooster dropped down upon him with claws and bill, and what the cat and dog had done to him was only a fly-bite to what that crook got from the rooster.

"Oh, save me! The place is haunted!" says the crooked thief, and he staggered out the door, down the steps, and into the hind legs of the donkey, which kicked that thief into the air and laid him out in the mud. As soon as that crooked captain was able, he crawled away, dragging one foot after another, till he reached the wood.

"Well, well," cried those crooked thieves, "any chance of our treasure?"

"Treasure! I was lucky to escape with my life! That house is cursed, I tell you, cursed! When I got to the kitchen fire to light a match, a witch leapt up and scratched my face. When I crossed the room a demon stuck his pitchfork into my legs. When I was passing through the door, it must be the devil himself that pounced down on me with his claws. Well, at last I escaped, only to have some imp smite me with a sledgehammer and send me sailing into the mud. If you don't believe me, go back there yourselves. I'm never going to that cursed place again!" And he didn't, and neither did the rest of them.

Well, the next morning Jack and his comrades were up before the sun. They made a hearty breakfast on what was left from the night before, and then they all agreed to go to town and give the magistrate the stolen treasure to return to the rightful owners. As a reward for recovering the treasure and driving out the crooks, Jack got the crooks' cabin, stable, and land, and a pile of gold and silver coins. He took those coins and away they went, Jack, donkey, dog, cat, and rooster, up hills, down dales, and sometimes along the high road, till they came to the gate of Jack's mother's old run-down cottage. Jack fetched his mother back to the cabin in the woods, where they made themselves to home.

The donkey and the dog and the rooster got the best places in the farmyard, and the cat took possession of the kitchen. Jack and his mother settled in comfortably, and as Jack always said, "Bless my soul! The more the merrier!" they all were as happy as could be.

King Hairy Goat Ears

Ages 6–9. Retold by Janice M. Del Negro from "The Goat's Ears of the Emperor Trojan," in _The Violet Fairy Book_ by Andrew Lang (Longmans, Green, 1910). Other versions of this tale can be found in a wide variety of cultures, from Greek myths to Irish folktales.

The key to a story like this, as with almost any tale in which the magical is part of the environment, is to tell the story as absolute truth, responding to each occurrence as if, although strange and bizarre, it is totally believable. Small physical gestures—such as your hands held aside your own ears to indicate the king's ears—make the teller visually interesting, and the occasional low-key goat bleat inserted when discussing the ears will be sure to get a laugh.

Once upon a time there lived a king who did not always do the smart thing. He had once insulted a powerful magician and as a result the king, well, the king had ears like a hairy goat. The king was very embarrassed by these ears because they not only proved he was stupid, they made him look like, well, a goat—so he tried to hide them the best he could, and no one in the kingdom was allowed to speak of them. Every morning, when he was shaved, the king asked the barbers, "Do you notice anything odd about me? Come now, I am your king, I demand the truth!" Well, the barbers didn't have much more sense than the king because they couldn't keep themselves from laughing when they said, "The king has hairy goat ears!" As each barber replied "The king has hairy goat ears!" he was put to death at once.

Now after this state of things had lasted a good long while, there was hardly a barber left in the kingdom, and it came to be the turn of the Master Barber to go up to the palace and shave the king. The Master Barber had noticed the loss of the kingdom's barbers, however, so he sent one of his apprentices to the king instead. The young barber was taken to the king's bedroom.

"Where is your master?" demanded the king.

"Your gracious majesty," replied the polite and quick-thinking young barber, "my master has a terrible cold, and rather than risk giving your majesty such a dreadful malady, he sent me, his own apprentice, since I am the only one he trusts with the honor of shaving your majesty."

The king was satisfied with this answer and sent everyone else out of the room. The king sat down, and the young barber began his work. He, like the rest of the barbers, noticed the king's hairy goat ears. How could he not notice? When the young barber finished, the king asked his usual question.

"Do you notice anything odd about me? Come now, I am your king, I demand the truth!" This young man, however, had a great deal of sense, and he replied calmly, "No, your majesty, nothing at all."

This pleased the king so much that he gave the young barber a pouch of gold coins and said, "Henceforth you shall be known as the Royal Barber and none but you shall shave me. Move into the palace, your fortune is made."

So when the apprentice barber returned home and the master inquired how he had got on with the king, the young man answered, "Oh, very well indeed! I have been named the Royal Barber, and I am to move into the palace and shave the king every day. My pockets are full of gold and my fortune is made." All this because he kept his mouth shut and said nothing—to anyone— about the king's hairy goat ears.

From this time on the young man shaved the king every day, receiving each morning a pouch of gold in payment. After a while though, his secret, which he carefully kept, weighed as heavily as a mountain of gold, and he longed to tell what he knew to somebody. The secret tormented him for months, until he could not eat, he could not sleep, he could hardly think of anything else. The young barber knew he should never feel easy until he shared his secret somehow. But who could he tell? He knew in his heart that a secret told was a secret no longer—but the secret of the king's hairy goat ears was becoming more than he could bear.

One afternoon the young man went walking in the countryside to get his mind off . . . you know. The walk in the countryside didn't help much; it was spring, and there were baby goats everywhere. Finally, the young man could bear it no longer. In the corner of a meadow he dug a deep hole. Then he knelt down and whispered into the hole three times over: "The king has hairy goat ears. The king has hairy goat ears. The king has hairy goat ears." As he whispered the words a great burden seemed to roll off him, and he shoveled the earth carefully back into the hole and ran lightly home.

Weeks went by, and the Royal Barber cheerfully shaved the king, and the secret was safely buried deep in the hole in the meadow. Some secrets demand to be told, however, and in the hole where the young barber had planted whispers there sprang up an elder tree. Some goatherds tending their flocks nearby noticed the tree growing there, and one of them cut down a stem to make a flute. The flute did not play melodies, however—no tender love songs, no sprightly dances, no soothing lullabies—no, the flute would do nothing but sing: "The king has hairy goat ears. The King Has Hairy Goat Ears! THE KING HAS HAIRY GOAT EARS!" Of course, it was not long before the whole kingdom knew of this elderwood flute and the tune it sang, and, at last, the news reached the king in his palace. The king was very upset. He trusted the young man. He was actually fond of him. He sent for the Royal Barber.

"What have you been saying about me to all my people?!?"

"Nothing, your majesty! Nothing! I haven't told anyone about your . . . I haven't told anyone anything! I swear!"

The king, instead of listening, only drew his sword from its sheath.

"Your majesty, wait! All I did was dig a hole!" The young barber told the king how he had whispered the truth three times to the earth, and how he had filled the hole and left lighter of heart.

"How was I to know that in that very place an elder tree would spring up! It's not my fault that a flute cut from that tree repeats the words I whispered into the ground!"

The king commanded his coach to be made ready. He grabbed the Royal Barber by the ear and bundled him into the coach. They drove to the spot, for the king wished to see for himself whether the young man's confession was true. When they reached the place, the king had his attendants cut him a flute from the elder tree, and, when it was ready, he ordered his chamberlain to play it. The chamberlain was the best flute player at court, but it didn't matter; no tune could he play. No matter how hard the chamberlain blew, nothing came out of the flute—no tender love songs, no sprightly dances, no soothing lullabies—nothing but the words, "The king has hairy goat ears. The King Has Hairy Goat Ears! THE KING HAS HAIRY GOAT EARS!"

The king was appalled. The king was embarrassed. The king was, to tell the truth, a little relieved. His secret was out. Now he knew that even the earth gave up its secrets, and perhaps that was for the best. The king granted the Royal Barber his life, and his position, and his fortune. For the rest of his life the king tried to be less of a silly goat than his ears made him appear.

— The Monkey, the Dog, and the Carabao —

Ages 6–9. Retold by Janice M. Del Negro from *Filipino Popular Tales* by Dean S. Fansler, as narrated by José M. Hilario, a Tagalog from Batangas, capital city of the province of Batangas (Folklore Associates, 1921).

The big-toothed giant in this story is called a Buṅgisṅgis in the Philippines and often has demonic or supernatural powers. A carabao is a type of domesticated Asian water buffalo.

Once there lived three friends, a monkey, a dog, and a carabao. They were tired of city life, so crowded and dangerous, and they decided to move to the country, where there were fewer people and life was peaceful. They took rice and meat, pots and pans, and spoons to stir the stew.

The first day the carabao was left at home to cook the food, so that the dog and the monkey would have something to eat when they returned from the hunt. After the monkey and the dog set off, the carabao began to rattle the pans, boil the rice, and fry the meat. Unfortunately the noise of the pans and the smell of the cooking meat attracted a big-toothed giant who lived in the forest. Seeing this chance to fill his stomach, the giant went up to the carabao and said, "Well, friend, I see that you have made me dinner."

"We are not friends, and this food is not for you. Go away and get your own dinner!"

This made the big-toothed giant angry, and he seized the carabao by the horn and threw him knee-deep into the earth. Then the big-toothed giant ate up all the food and disappeared.

When the monkey and the dog came home, everything was a terrible mess, and their friend was still knee-deep in the ground.

"Oh, friend, what has happened to you?" cried the monkey and the dog.

The monkey and the dog pulled the carabao out of the ground and brushed him off.

"Giant! Big teeth! Before I knew it he threw me into the ground. And then he ate all the food I prepared for our dinner!"

"There, there," said the dog. "Do not worry. We caught more food for our dinner."

"There, there," said the monkey. "We will cook our meal together."

The three friends then rattled the pans, boiled the rice, and fried the meat. The sounds and smells of the cooking spread through the forest. The big-toothed giant heard the sounds and smelled the smells and his belly rumbled, but he did not dare attack all three of them at once.

The next day the dog was left behind to cook so that the monkey and the carabao would have something to eat when they returned from the hunt. The dog rattled the pans, boiled the rice, and fried the meat. The big-toothed giant heard the sounds and smelled the smells, and he went up to the dog and said, "Well, friend, I see that you have made me dinner."

"We are not friends, and this food is not for you," said the dog. "Go away and get your own dinner!"

The dog snarled, the big-toothed giant roared, and he seized the dog by the tail and threw him knee-deep into the earth. The dog could not cry to his companions for help, for, if he did, the big-toothed giant would surely kill him. So he watched his unwelcome guest eat all of the food. Then the big-toothed giant disappeared.

Soon after the big-toothed giant's departure, the monkey and the carabao returned.

"Oh, friend, what has happened to you?"

The monkey and the carabao pulled the dog out of the ground and brushed him off.

"Giant! Big teeth! Before I knew it he threw me into the ground. And then he ate all the food I prepared for our dinner!"

The monkey and the carabao were angry to learn that the big-toothed giant had been there again, but they comforted their friend the dog.

"There, there," said the carabao. "Do not worry. We caught more food for our dinner."

"There, there," said the monkey. "We will cook our meal together."

The three friends rattled the pans, boiled the rice, and fried the meat. The sounds and smells of the cooking spread through the forest. The big-toothed giant heard the sounds and smelled the smells, and his belly rumbled, but he was too afraid to attack all three of them at once.

The next day the monkey was cook. He was a good cook, and a wise monkey. Before cooking he dug a pit in front of the stove. After putting away enough food for his companions and himself, he rattled the pans, boiled the rice, and fried the meat. The big-toothed giant heard the sounds and smelled the smells, and his belly rumbled. He went up to the monkey and said, "Well, friend, I see that you have made me dinner."

The monkey, very politely, said, "Sir, you have come just in time. Please, sit down, dinner is ready."

The big-toothed giant gladly accepted the offer, and, after sitting down in a chair, began to devour the food. When the big-toothed giant was busy eating, the monkey took hold of a leg of the chair, gave it a yank, and sent the big-toothed giant tumbling into the pit. The monkey then filled the pit with earth, so that the big-toothed giant was covered and captured. "There," said the monkey. "Magic you may be, but the earth holds you just the same."

When the monkey's companions arrived, they asked about the big-toothed giant. At first the monkey did not tell them what had happened, but they kept asking and kept asking until he finally told them that the big-toothed giant was buried in front of the stove. Curious and foolish, the dog and the carabao dug up the pit, and the big-toothed giant jumped out with a great roar! The dog and the carabao raced away, but the monkey, as was his nature, climbed up a tree. In the branches of the tree was a beehive, sitting on top of a vine.

"Now I'll certainly kill you," said the big-toothed giant, coming toward the monkey.

"Spare me," said the monkey, "and I will give up my place to you."

"What place is that?" asked the big-toothed giant.

"Ah! Did you not know? I am the royal bell ringer. My job is to ring each hour of the day on this bell up here." Monkey pointed to the beehive on top of the vine. "Every time I ring the bell, I get a silver coin."

"I would like some silver coins, all right!" said the big-toothed giant. "I accept the position."

"Stay here while I find out what time it is," said the monkey. The monkey scampered down the tree and joined his friends in the woods. The monkey, the dog, and the carabao watched and waited. The minutes buzzed by.

"Where is that monkey?" said the big-toothed giant. "It must be time to ring the bell!" Impatient, the big-toothed giant pulled the vine. The beehive fell out of the tree onto the ground. Crash! A swarm of angry bees surrounded the big-toothed giant, and buzzing and stinging, they drove him deep into the forest. The dog and the carabao and the monkey watched bees and giant disappear into the trees.

"Well, friends," said the monkey, "the big-toothed giant may never return. Or then again, he might. Perhaps city life was not so bad."

The dog and the carabao agreed, and the three friends moved out of the quiet, dangerous country back to the safety of the crowded, noisy city, where they rattled the pans, boiled the rice, and fried the meat, but never again attracted the attention of a big-toothed giant.

CHAPTER 4

SURPRISE AND LAUGHTER

Ages 9 to 12

My students are always surprised that finding a story they want to tell is so much more difficult than they anticipate. Start by reading a wide variety of folktales in compilations and single-tale volumes. Look for the stories that appeal to you and that you think might appeal to your listeners. Stories that appeal to adult sensibilities are not always successful with young listeners, so remember to whom you will be telling. Read each story aloud to get a sense of how the story works when told out loud, not read silently. This exercise will also help you judge how long the story really is, where the slow spots that may need adjusting are located, and whether the version you are reading has enough action or emotion to hold your listeners.

When you are reading aloud, read as dramatically as you can. Overstate the suspense, excitement, or silliness; this will help you determine the emotional content of the story, which will enable you to evoke those emotions both in your delivery and in your listeners. A key to story selection and delivery is to decide how you want your listeners to feel about the story when you are finished telling it.

Choosing the right type of tale for the listening audience can be tricky. Younger listeners have to be invited into story and gain experience about how story works. Older listeners, starting roughly around fourth grade, with any luck have not only responded to the invitation, they are usually ready for nearly any type of effectively told tale. Just as transitional readers are ready for more sophisticated concepts, so are 9- to 12-year-old story listeners ready for more sophisticated stories. Very generally speaking, once children reach the elementary and middle grades, the range of stories for telling increases exponentially.

Elementary-age listeners are ready for more complex plots with more complex emotional subtexts; they are very concerned with friendship and with unity or success against the odds, or both, and they enjoy stories that feature admirable heroes and heroines. This does not necessarily mean those between 9 and 12 years old want serious tales about serious concerns; this age is particularly responsive to the funny or clever tale. They are also very fond of the supernatural or gory story. Actually, nearly every age group, including adults, is fond of the supernatural or gory story, so having at least a few in your repertoire can never hurt. Myths, legends, magic, and ghosts—all are suitable places to begin with this age group (for example, "Molly Whuppie," "Damon and Pythias," and similar tales with a strong dramatic arc). As a beginning teller you are building a repertoire, so look for stories you can tell often, to a fairly disparate age range. Once you start telling to older listeners, stories with a wide range of appeal are easier to come by. The tale that works for all ages, what is often called the general family audience tale, is a boon to every storyteller. When you find one it will become an essential part of your repertoire. "Jack and the Haunted House," an Appalachian ghost tale, is one such story; so is "Tailypo," a jump tale from the American South, which is the StoryCoaching tale for this chapter. A jump tale is a story in which the storyteller manipulates pace and volume in order to surprise listeners into an involuntary, collective response.

Children in this age group will sit for longer, more complicated stories, especially if they've been exposed to storytelling before. They are developing a taste for the odd and strange—they do like tales with elements of the gross and disgusting—that will last well into junior high and high school. They are curious and enjoy jokes and are beginning to understand sarcasm. Listeners of this age are starting to develop ideas about the world, can understand other points of view, and are capable of empathy. What you tell depends on your connection to your audience members and their ability to be creative listeners.

Stories for ages 9 to 12 tend to be more complex and require an approach different from that used for the simple cumulative tales used with younger listeners. Tellers to this age group cannot depend on audience participation to carry the story; in fact, participation falls off precipitously with this age group. They are extremely concerned about the opinions of their peers and unlikely to engage in anything that will make them look silly. Fourth graders are more likely to participate than fifth graders (especially if they are grouped with younger listeners), while fifth graders are looking to sixth graders for behavior models, and sixth graders often will not engage in what they consider babyish behavior (that is, participating in stories). They are not interested in being cute; they are interested in being cool.

Many storytelling how-to books have suggestions for how to learn a story. Widely respected librarian, storyteller, and folklorist Margaret Read MacDonald includes a section in her book *Storyteller's Start-Up Book* (August House, 2006) on how to learn a story in an hour. Every storyteller learns differently: some tellers write a bullet list of plot points and phrases; some draw story maps with simple stick figures and lollipop trees to reflect the action; some use flash cards; some imagine the story as a movie in their heads. There are as many ways to learn a story as there are storytellers.

Learning a more complex folktale for telling does not require memorization; in fact, memorization can be a problem. If you are too text-bound you can easily get lost in your own story. Instead, internalize the chronology of events. When practicing a story, practice the whole story; learn it whole, not in pieces. To paraphrase the King in *Alice in Wonderland*, when learning a story *begin at the beginning, go on till the end, and then stop*. Always know what is going to happen next and where the story needs to end, and you will not get lost. Perfection is neither expected nor required; the listening ear is very forgiving, as long as the chronology of events is clear.

In the early days of library storytelling, the storyteller was transparent; that is, he or she was merely the conduit for the tale. My first official storytelling teacher, Margaret Poarch, was emphatic on this point: it is the story that matters, not the storyteller. Learn the story well, and then trust the story to do what it has done for centuries of listeners. To this I would add that librarian storytellers must tell stories in their most authentic voice, from the center of their most authentic selves. Put simply, be yourself. My strong suggestion is to find several variants of a tale and combine them to create your own. Two indispensable tools for researching and finding tales and tale variants are Judy Sierra's *The Storyteller's Research Guide: Folktales, Myths, and Legends*, and Margaret Read MacDonald's two editions of *The Storyteller's Sourcebook*.

Remember there is no such thing as the definitive version of a folktale; the story you find in one book is just one version of that story. Some versions of folktales are flat, their energy lost to a dryly written retelling; they need the voice, inflection, and physicality of the storyteller to make them live. Tales that are heavily narrative can usually benefit from the addition of dialogue; don't tell your listeners what is happening, show them through conversation between or among characters. This gives you the chance to give your characters vivid personalities. Librarian and storyteller Carol Birch includes many ways to add dimension to characters in her book *The Whole Story Handbook*.

There are many different models of oral and written narrative structure, but for the purposes of this book we are concentrating on traditional linear narrative (events proceeding in chronological order), as it has been my experience that this is the most effective form of oral narrative for both the listening audience and the storyteller learning the story. Here is the best way I have found to describe the structure of an effective oral story: introduction; initial incident, problem, or conflict; plot development; climax; and conclusion. What follows is a very general outline of that structure using as an example an abbreviated version of the tale of "The Golden Goose" by the Grimm Brothers.

Introduction

Once upon a time in a cottage in the woods there lived an old woodcutter and his three sons.

The introduction tells the listeners when they are ("once upon a time"), where they are ("in a cottage in the woods"), and who the characters are ("there lived an old woodcutter and his three sons"). Notice that the listeners get all this information in the first line of the story; keep the narrative simple and clean.

Initial Incident, Problem, or Conflict

One day the oldest son decided to go into the forest and chop some firewood. The old woodcutter gave his oldest son a fine lunch of savory meat and sweet cider, and the young man set out. When he entered the forest, the oldest son met an old man.

This is the beginning of the action, the setup for what is going to follow. The oldest son refuses to share his meal with the old man, and when the son lifts his ax he is injured and must return home. The same thing happens to the second son. The third son, who has only a pitiful lunch of bread and water, readily agrees to share with the old man. Upon opening his bag, the youngest son finds savory meat and sweet cider.

Plot Development

After a satisfying meal, the old man said to the youngest son, "Take your ax and chop down this tree, and see what you will find there." The old man disappeared, and the youngest son took his ax and cut down the tree. There, on the stump of the tree, was a goose with feathers of gold. Not just the color of gold, but real gold! The youngest son thought, "Well! A young man with a golden goose must seek whatever fortune lies ahead." Tucking the goose under his arm, the youngest son set off for town.

Plot development includes the rising action and the logical sequence of events; that is, the action of the story takes off here. Sometimes, as in the case of this youngest son, the hero takes off on a literal journey that includes various incidents or adventures. This youngest son's adventures include stopping at an inn and discovering that anyone who tries to steal feathers from the goose will stick to it; the youngest son then wends his way to town followed by the innkeeper's three daughters, a priest, a sexton, a farmer, and others—a veritable, if unwilling, parade of people.

Climax

The youngest son entered the town square on market day, golden goose under his arm, followed by the three sisters, the priest, the sexton, the farmer, and everyone else acquired during the journey. On a balcony overlooking the market square sat the princess, the only daughter of the king of all the land. Now this princess had never laughed, and her father the king had promised that anyone who could make her laugh would get a wagon full of gold and two fine horses to draw it. The princess took one look at the youngest son, the golden goose honking under his arm, and the parade of people following and without a thought burst into laughter. Her laugh broke the golden goose's enchantment, and the parade of people, much relieved, hastened to their homes.

The climax of the story is the highest point of interest, the place where everything that has gone before comes to fruition. The solution to the problem or conflict is achieved. This is, for all intents and purposes, the end of the story; everything after this is simply wrap-up for the sake of satisfactory closure.

Conclusion

The king was delighted that his daughter had found her smile, and the youngest son quickly had his wagon full of gold and two fine horses to draw it. Where he traveled after that, well, that is another story!

The conclusion should come quickly after the climax of the tale, tie up any remaining loose ends, and deliver a sense of satisfaction.

This story structure applies to many forms of traditional linear narrative; in fact, it applies to written linear narrative as well. For example, if you decide you want to tell a personal or historical tale, this structure works well for organizing the sequence of narrative events. Once you internalize this structure, once you are comfortable with the parts of successful linear oral narrative, you will find it easier to learn and deliver a wide variety of tales.

The supernatural or gory story is wildly popular with nearly every listener at nearly every age; you will get an audience for scary tales when you cannot get an audience for any other kind of storytelling event. There will occasionally be those who are not interested or do not approve of the supernatural or gory tale, so it is important to be very clear when you are offering this type of program. Make sure all publicity and program descriptions emphasize the content and appropriate ages for the program. When you introduce the program, tell the attendees what the content will be: "Tonight we are telling scary tales for ages 9 to 12. This program is not recommended for any listener under age 9 or anyone who does not appreciate the traditional scary story." The tremendous popularity of this type of tale cannot be underestimated, so make sure you have a book display and booklist to go with your program. There is no reason to do any programming that does not promote the services and resources of the library. Make the connections from the stories being told to the texts, audiobooks, e-books, programs, and other resources available to your patrons.

———— STORYCOACHING ————

"Tailypo, a Jump Tale," retold by Janice M. Del Negro from multiple print and oral sources, including Joel Chandler Harris's *Uncle Remus Returns* (Houghton Mifflin, 1918) in which it is actually part of a longer Brer Rabbit story.

"Tailypo" is a jump tale from the American South. Think of the moment in the horror movie after the scary music fades and all seems well; suddenly,

the monster leaps out of the closet and the audience members jump in their seats. A jump tale is a story in which the storyteller manipulates pace and volume in order to surprise listeners into an involuntary, collective response. "Tailypo" is a popular gory story that can work with a fairly wide range of ages, depending on whether the storyteller emphasizes the humor or the suspense.

On the edge of the woods on the edge of a swamp in the deep middle of Louisiana there once lived an ornery old man. This old man lived in a one-room cabin with his three hunting dogs, Not Real Good, Almost Bad, and Good Enough. Now this old man lived on whatever he could hunt, and one day on the edge of a winter morning he went out to hunt something to eat. He called to his dogs, "Not Real Good! Almost Bad! Good Enough!" and went into the woods looking for something for dinner. The old man and his dogs hunted all day, but all the old man caught was one skinny rabbit. Well, something was something and not nothing, so the old man took the rabbit home, skinned it, cooked it, ate it, and gave the bones to the dogs.

Open in a matter-of-fact manner, as if you are backed by the authoritative truth of this story. The rhythm and pace of the language are important to setting up the suspenseful moments that will follow.

The old man was still hungry, and so were the dogs, but nothing is nothing and not something, so the old man pulled his rocking chair up close to the fire and decided to snooze his hunger away. His eyes were just closing when he got a feeling. You know that feeling? That one moment you're alone in a room and the next moment you know you're not?

Invite your listeners in through this possible shared experience. Talk to them as if they are old enough to have had and survived a scary event.

The old man didn't move so's you'd notice, just let his half-closed eyes roam around the one-room cabin—and there it was. Some kind of critter, an animal that the old man had never seen before, had crept into the cabin through a crack in the wall along with the wind. The animal was about the size of a giant possum, and it had a long, skinny tail.

Pause before the word "critter"—the pause will catch listeners' attention, and draw them to you. Form the size of the critter in the air with your hands; indicate the length of the tail the same way.

The old man moved really slow, reached down beside his rocking chair, and grabbed hold of the handle of his ax. Quick as a flash he threw that ax at the critter in the cabin.

When the narrative says "The old man moved really slow," slow down the pace of your telling and lower the volume of your voice; with the words "quick as a flash," pick up the pace and volume. Point in front of you to the place the ax lands.

And he hit it! Not all of it though; just its tail. The critter skittered through the crack in the cabin wall, leaving its tail behind.

After "And he hit it!" pause for a moment for the anticlimax of "Not all of it though; just its tail." This is a good "ewwww!" moment.

The old man got up, walked over to the tail, and picked it up.

Pick up the tail with thumb and forefinger. Hold it out to the side and look at it for a moment.

The tail was long and skinny. The tail was scaly and hairy. The old man had never seen anything like this tail before, and he had seen plenty. Still, something was something and not nothing, so the old man took the tail, skinned it, cooked it, ate it, and gave the bones to the dogs.

Look the tail up and down. Look at listeners when saying "The old man had never seen anything like this tail before, and he had seen plenty" while still holding the tail out to the side. After "Still, something was something and not nothing," wipe your hands and shrug your shoulders to indicate acceptance of the inevitable. This is another good "ewww!" moment.

Now the old man and his dogs had full stomachs, and a warm fire to sleep in front of, so, after the old man had stuffed the crack in the cabin wall with rags, that's what they did. The old man fell asleep in his rocking chair, and the dogs in front of the fire.

Indicate the drowsy warmth by slowing down and lowering your voice. You might even give a little snore.

The wind from the swamp howled around the cabin and on the wind came a moaning sound: "Tailypo . . . tailypo . . . you know and I know that I need my tailypo."

Keep your voice low and smooth. Whisper the phrase slowly, almost sing it, giving particular emphasis to the word "need."

The old man flung the cabin door open, and called to his dogs, "Not Real Good! Almost Bad! Good Enough!" The dogs scrambled out the cabin door and chased that thing back into the swamp.

Raise your voice, pick up the pace, and make this sound just a touch frantic.

When the dogs came back the old man made them sleep under the porch, so's they could watch over the cabin. The old man banked the fire for the night and climbed into his bed. He hadn't even closed his eyes when skriiitch! Skriiitch! He heard something scratching on the cabin door: "Tailypo, my tailypo, you know and I know that I want my tailypo."

Make your voice low and rough and slowly draw out the "skriiitch! Skriiitch!"

The old man hollered for the dogs. "Not Real Good! Almost Bad! Good Enough!" and the dogs they scrambled out from under the porch and chased that thing back into the swamp.

Again, this should be hurried and frightened. Pause after the dogs chase the creature back into the swamp.

The old man sat up in bed for awhile, but soon his eyes got droopy, and he laid his head on his pillow. He was just drifting off when skriiitch! Skriiitch!

Make your voice low and rough and slowly draw out the "skriiitch! Skriiitch!"

Claws scrabbled across the roof of the cabin, and the moaning voice came down the chimney: "Tailypo, tailypo, you know and I know that I need my tailypo."

The creature's voice can be low and growly, liquid and feline, or whatever you are most comfortable with; whatever you choose, the creature must be very "other." Decide what works best for you.

The old man hollered for the dogs right from his bed. "Not Real Good! Almost Bad! Good Enough!" The dogs didn't come. The old man hollered again. "Not Real Good! Almost Bad! Good Enough!" But the dogs didn't come. See, the last time the dogs chased that critter into the swamp, that critter had led those dogs deep, deep into the cypress, and lost them there.

This is where the storyteller begins to set up the jump. The pace slows, the delivery becomes more deliberate. You are foreshadowing the end. Your voice should be quiet and matter of fact. While the old man is frightened, the storyteller is calm.

The old man was all alone. He was so scared, he couldn't even get out of bed. He pulled the covers over his head, closed his eyes, and wished for morning. He closed his eyes so tight and wished so long, he finally fell asleep, and when he woke up, that critter was sitting at the foot of the bed.

Pause briefly after "and when he woke up." Point to the foot of the bed, somewhere around the center of your listening audience.

The old man could see that critter's red eyes glowing in the moonlight coming through the window. "What . . . what do you want?" the old man asked.

The old man's voice shakes here.

The critter blinked. "You know and I know that I want my tailypo."

The creature's voice is low and threatening.

The old man sat up in bed, the covers around his chin. "I don't have your tailypo," he said desperately. "I'd give it to you if I could." The critter uncurled, and began to walk up the old man's body, until it was sitting right on his chest. The old man could feel the critter's hot breath on his cheek.

Use your hands to indicate the creature walking up the old man's body; place your two hands on your chest to indicate where the creature stops. Your voice should be deeper, your pace deliberate.

"You know and I know that I want my tailypo."

Your volume must be close to normal here. The repetitive phrases should be delivered in a low, singsong rhythm.

"You know and I know that I want my tailypo."

Lower the volume on the second phrase.

"You know and I know that I want my tailypo."

Lower the volume further on the third phrase.

"And I know how to GET IT!"

Drop the volume to a whisper on "And I know how to . . ." and raise it quickly and emphatically on ". . . GET IT!" while stepping forward and throwing your hands, curved into claws, out abruptly. The whisper will draw listeners in, while the abrupt change in volume and the forward motion will make them jump. The success of the jump is dependent upon the setup, the deliberate control of volume and pace.

And that critter tore up everything in the room: the rocking chair, the bed . . . the old man.

This should be stated very matter-of-factly. Take a long pause to let the old man's fate sink in. Then, low and slow, and a little regretful . . .

Some say that if you go back to the woods on the edge of that cypress swamp, you can see what's left of that old cabin. It's empty now. Some say the old man and the dogs disappeared into the swamp. Some say he just moved where there were less mosquitoes.

Deliver this at regular volume, at a fairly quick pace, as if repeating gossip.

But some say that if you go to the cabin in the woods at the edge of the swamp, on a near winter night when the moon is high, if you stand very still and listen very hard, you can hear a moan on the wind, coming from the swamp. "Tailypo, my tailypo, you know and I know that I got my tailypo."

Slow down a little here; go back to the low voice and deliberate pace of the encounter between man and creature. Deliver that final "Tailypo, my tailypo, you know and I know that I got my tailypo" in a satisfied singsong.

Tales-to-Text: Suggestions for Independent Readers

Alley, Zoe B. *There's a Princess in the Palace*. Roaring Brook, 2010.

Berner, Rotraut Susanne. *Definitely Not for Little Ones: Very Grimm Fairy-Tale Comics*. Trans. by Shelley Tanaka. Groundwood Books, 2009.

"The Big Hairy Tale." In *Jackie Tales* by Jackie Torrence. Avon, 1998.

Bunting, Eve. *Finn McCool and the Great Fish: A Story about Acquiring Wisdom*. Sleeping Bear, 2010.

"Chunk o' Meat." In *Grandfather Tales* by Richard Chase. Houghton, 1948, pp. 40–51.

Galdone, Joanna. *The Tailypo: A Ghost Story*. Illus. by Paul Galdone. Clarion, 1977.

"The Golden Goose." In *About Wise Men and Simpletons: Twelve Tales from the Brothers Grimm*. Trans. by Elizabeth Shub, illus. by Nonny Hogrogrian. MacMillan, 1971.

Hamilton, Martha, and Mitch Weiss. *The Ghost Catcher: A Bengali Folktale*. August House, 2008.

Jolley, Dan. *Pigling: A Cinderella Story: A Korean Tale*. Pencils and inks by Anne Timmons. Graphic Universe, 2009.

Kajikawa, Kimiko. *Tsunami!* Illus. by Ed Young. Philomel Books, 2009.

Kirby, Ellie. *The Big Toe: An Appalachian Ghost Story.* Fox Creek, 2010.

Lunge-Larsen, Lise. *The Race of the Birkebeiners.* Houghton Mifflin, 2001.

Medearis, Angela Shelf. *Tailypo: A Newfangled Tall Tale.* Illus. by Sterling Brown. Holiday House, 1996.

Mitchell, Marianne. *Joe Cinders.* Henry Holt, 2002.

"My Big Toe." In *Diane Goode's Book of Scary Stories and Songs.* Puffin Books, 1994.

O'Malley, Kevin. *Velcome.* Walker, 1997.

"The Peculiar Such Thing." Retold by Virginia Hamilton. In *The People Could Fly: American Black Folktales.* Illus. by Leo and Diane Dillon. Knopf, 1985.

Sharpe, Leah Marinsky. *The Goat-Faced Girl: A Classic Italian Folktale.* David R. Godine, 2009.

"Tailypo." Told by Jackie Torrence, a prominent North Carolina story-teller. Video recording can be viewed and downloaded at the Book-Hive website, Charlotte Mecklenburg Library, Charlotte, North Carolina, www.cmlibrary.org/bookhive/zingertales/default.asp?storyid=6.

Ungar, Richard. *Even Higher.* Tundra Books, 2007.

Wahl, Jan. *Tailypo!* Illus. by Wil Clay. Henry Holt, 1991.

Washington, Donna. *A Big Spooky House.* Jump at the Sun, 2000.

Four Friends and a Lion

Ages 9–12. Retold by Janice M. Del Negro from *The World's Best Literature,*
Volume 19, edited by Charles Dudley Warner, John William Cunliffe, et al.
(Knickerbocker/Warner Library, 1917), and *Entertainer and Entertained*,
compiled by Eleanor H. Caldwell (Mayhew Publishing, 1911).

This tale from ancient India is from the classic work known as the Pan-
chatantra, collections of animal fables in poetry and prose that include the
Buddhist Jataka tales. This particular story is often anthologized as "The
Lion-makers" or "The Four Brahmins and the Lion."

The scene in which the learned men speak the words of power must be told
in a tone of majesty and awe, because the humor of this story lies in the
contrast between the self-importance of the learned men and the common
sense of the farmer's son.

There were once four friends who grew up in the same village.
Three of the friends came from wealthy families, but one young
man was a farmer's son, and not nearly so well off. When the boys
were young, this disparity did not matter, for fishing and tramping
through the jungle cost little, but when the boys grew older, well,
the opportunities for farmers' sons were not the same as for sons
of wealthy men. The three wealthy friends were sent to the city

to go to university and learn about the world, while the farmer's son stayed home and learned about dirt: when to plant, when to harvest, when to lie fallow.

Years went by, and the three sons of wealthy fathers returned from the city, where they had become learned men, educated in the ways of art, science, and magic. The farmer's son? He knew a lot about dirt. And worms. And the cycles of the seasons. The three learned men were only home to visit before they set out to make their mark on the world. They visited with the farmer's son and felt deep pity for him.

"See here," said one. "Our friend is far behind us, it is true, but he is our friend. Let us invite him on this journey with us, for otherwise he will never learn what is important in the world. Besides, we need someone to carry the packs."

So the three learned men invited their old friend to travel with them, and, after talking to his father and his grandfather, the farmer's son decided to go and see the world. The four friends set out, with the farmer's son carrying the packs, for after all, he was not wise in the ways of the university and so had to contribute some other way.

The men had not been traveling long when they came across the bones of a lion lying in the middle of the path. The first learned man stepped forward.

"In my studies I have learned much about the world. I have learned the words that will shape these bones just as they were when the lion lived."

The first learned man approached the bones on the path, held his hands over them, and spoke the words. The jungle noises faded, and the words the learned man spoke crackled over the bones of the lion and behold! On the path was the skeleton of a lion, just as it had been in life. The second learned man stepped forward.

"In my studies I have learned much. I have discovered the words that will put muscle, flesh, and fur upon the bones of this lion, just as they were when the lion lived."

The second learned man stepped forward, held his hands over the lion's skeleton, and spoke. His words cracked like lightning around the lion's skeleton, and behold! The bones were covered with muscle, flesh, and fur, just as they had been in life.

The third learned man stepped forward.

"My studies have led me into dark and secret places, places where few dare to venture. In my studies I have learned the words that will breathe life back into the bones and flesh and fur of this lion."

The third learned man stepped forward, held out his hands, and . . .

"Wait!" cried the farmer's son. The three learned men looked at their old friend.

"That is a lion." The farmer's son spoke slowly.

The three learned men looked at their old friend with pity.

"Yes," they said soothingly. "We know."

The third learned man held out his hands and prepared to speak the words.

"Wait!" cried the farmer's son. "Just . . . let me climb this tree."

The farmer's son dropped the packs and climbed nimbly into the branches of a tree overhanging the path. The three learned friends smiled knowingly, and the third learned man held his hands over the lion in the path and spoke the words.

The words trembled on every hair on the lion's fur, and then . . . the lion breathed. He stretched out his paws like a great house cat, arched his back, shook his mane, took a deep breath, and roared till the birds trembled from the trees. The lion opened his great jaws . . . and ate the three learned men.

When the very full lion had padded down the path into the jungle, the farmer's son climbed down from the tree, picked up the packs, and went home. There he put into practice everything he knew about dirt, and so he lived a long and healthy life.

Liver

Ages 9–12. Retold by Janice M. Del Negro from urban legends and a variety of folk sources. A traditional version of this tale can be found in Otto Knoop's "Die kleine Geschichte," *Ostmärkische Sagen, Märchen und Erzählunge* (Lissa in Posen: Oskar Eulitz Verlag, 1909). This and other traditional versions of this story can be found at A Corpse Claims Its Property, folklore scholar D. L. Ashliman's inspirational website (www.pitt.edu/~dash/type0366.html).

This is a modified jump tale, a story in which the storyteller manipulates pace and volume in order to surprise listeners into an involuntary, collective response. The more conversational you make it, the more the humor will come through. The jump is set up just before the fourth ghostly refrain, "The sun baked it, the crows ate it, the wind . . . YOU HAVE IT!"

Once there was a guy and a girl. They were sweethearts. In fact, she called him Sweetcakes and he called her Honey Pie. Don't ask. Now Honey Pie loved to eat liver more than anything else in the world. Hard to imagine, but there it was. She simply could not live if she did not eat liver every single day. Her Sweetcakes was an understanding sort and pretty much went to town every day to fetch fresh liver from the butcher so that Honey Pie might have her heart's desire—liver—every single day.

One day, however, on his liver-fetching errand the young Sweetcakes ran into some friends, and instead of going to the butcher, he went to the café, where he ate and drank until his friends and his coins were gone.

Sad, and a little anxious because Honey Pie was not going to be happy that he was coming home late and without the liver, Sweet-cakes made his way toward Honey Pie's house. The sad young man was walking slowly through the forest when he met a hunter.

"Well, friend, I have seen many a downcast soul, but none more so than you," said the hunter. "Whatever ails you?"

"I am not ailing," said the young man, "but my Honey Pie soon will be. I have failed to get her heart's desire."

"What is that, then?" asked the hunter. "Jewels? Poetry? Eternal love?"

"No, . . . liver!" sobbed Sweetcakes.

The hunter thought for a moment and then said, "Well, my boy, I have a solution for you, but you will have to be very practical about it."

"Oh, anything to get my Honey Pie's heart's desire!" cried Sweetcakes.

"Not far along this path is the crossroads and at that crossroads is a gallows. On those gallows dangle the dead bodies of outlaws hung by their necks as a warning to others considering a life of crime."

Even Sweetcakes could see where this was going. The hunter continued.

"Take one of those bodies down, cut out his liver, and give it to your Honey Pie. Tell her it's beef. She won't know the difference."

Sweetcakes did not want to know how the hunter knew that, but Sweetcakes was nothing if not practical, and he was bound to get Honey Pie her heart's desire—so he went to the crossroads, cut down an outlaw, sliced out his liver, and brought it home to Honey Pie. The sun was setting by the time he got home.

"What took you so long in town, Sweetcakes?" said Honey Pie, not so sweetly. Honey Pie was pretty angry because Sweetcakes had been away so long.

"Oh, Honey Pie, I have such a treat for you! Fresh beef liver!"

Honey Pie's anger faded just a little when she saw that dark red liver. Sweetcakes knew just what to do.

"Here, my Honey Pie," he said. "Sit in the parlor and rest your feet. I will cook your liver, you don't have to do a thing."

Honey Pie went and put her feet up and then she snoozed right off.

Sweetcakes diced up some onions, warmed up the skillet, and fried up that liver. The smell filled the house, and Honey Pie's mouth began to water, even in her sleep.

Suddenly a white figure appeared at the kitchen window, and it cried into the room, "Honey Pie is asleep. The moon rises in the sky. And there you stand, frying my liver."

Sweetcakes was terrified. "Honey Pie, honey, is that you?" But Honey Pie snoozed on.

The latch on the kitchen door began to rattle, and the phantom, a white skeleton with a crooked neck, called out again.

"Honey Pie is asleep. The moon rises in the sky. And there you stand, frying my liver."

Sweetcakes could barely breathe. The kitchen door swung open and the skeleton stood shining in the doorway.

Sweetcakes took a breath and trembling all over asked, "Stand back, oh boney bandit, what happened to your flesh?"

The ghost replied, "The sun baked it, the crows ate it, and the wind blew it away."

Sweetcakes took a trembling breath and asked, "Stand back, oh boney bandit, what happened to your eyes?"

The ghost moaned, "The sun baked them, the crows ate them, and the wind blew them away."

Sweetcakes took another breath and asked, "Stand back, oh boney bandit, what happened to your ears?"

The ghost answered, "The sun baked them, the crows ate them, and the wind blew them away."

Sweetcakes could not help himself, he just had to ask. "Stand back, oh boney bandit, what happened to your . . . liver?"

The ghost moaned, "The sun baked it, the crows ate it, the wind . . . YOU HAVE IT!"

The skeleton got a liver to replace the one he lost—not his own liver, but there it is. Oh, Honey Pie? She never did get her heart's desire that night. She found another sweetie, though. Called him Sugarpot. Don't ask.

—— The Demon Goblin of Adachigahara ——

Ages 9–12. Retold by Janice M. Del Negro from *Japanese Fairy Tales*, compiled by
Yei Theodora Ozaki (A. L. Burt Company, 1908).

This straightforward chase-and-escape horror tale has a rising sense of fore-boding. For the general narrative the pace should move relatively quickly, the volume should be steady; the story really takes off when the main character gets to the cottage on the plain. Pace is very important in stories like this: once the pilgrim priest finds shelter, he falls into a false sense of security, so the pace can be gentle and lulling, the volume soft; as soon as he realizes his danger, the pace must pick up speed, and the intensity must increase for the howls of the demon goblin.

Long ago, in the province of Mutsu in Japan, there was a sweeping plain called Adachigahara. From time to time travelers crossing this plain vanished into the vast, open space and were never heard from again. The old women warming themselves at the charcoal braziers in the evenings and the young girls washing the household rice at the wells in the mornings whispered dreadful stories. The missing travelers had been devoured by a yokai, they said, a demon goblin that lived on human flesh. No one dared cross the plain after sunset; hardly anyone dared cross it in the noonday sun. Those who met unwary travelers warned them away from the awful place.

One day a priest came to the plain, a pilgrim walking from shrine to shrine to pray for a blessing. The sun was gone and the moon was hidden, so the plain was very dark, and the young priest had lost his way. The night was so late he met no one who could warn him not to cross the plain.

The pilgrim priest was tired and hungry. After wandering for hours he saw a clump of trees rise up in the distance, and through the trees he saw a single ray of light.

"Oh, praise to heaven! Surely that is a place I can shelter from the night!"

He forced his cold and aching feet toward the light, and soon came to a tumble-down cottage with a broken bamboo fence. The paper screens over the windows and doors were full of holes. The door to the hut was open, however, and by the light of an old lantern an old woman sat spinning.

The pilgrim called to her across the broken fence.

"Good evening, Oba-San! Please excuse me, but I have lost my way and have nowhere to rest tonight. I beg you to be good enough to let me shelter under your roof."

The old woman stopped spinning and looked at the young priest.

"I am very sorry you have lost your way in such a lonely spot, but I have no bed to offer you, and cannot host a guest."

"Oh," said the priest, "I would be grateful for even a spot on your floor. Please, it so cold."

The old woman was very reluctant, but at last she said, "Very well, I offer you welcome as my guest. Come in, I will make a fire to warm the house."

The old woman lit the fire.

"Come close to the fire and warm yourself," said the old woman. "You must be hungry. I will cook some rice, for it is all I have to offer."

After the priest ate his rice he and the old woman sat in front of the fire and talked while the night passed. The priest thought he had been very lucky to come across such a kind old woman in the middle of this deserted place.

"I will go out and gather some firewood," said the old woman finally, "for we have used it all. You must stay and take care of the house while I am gone."

"No, no," said the pilgrim, "let me gather the wood, for you are old, and I cannot let you go out on this cold night!"

The old woman shook her head.

"You must rest quietly here, for you are a guest in my house. Sit where you are and do not move. Whatever happens, do not go into the other room, for it is not fit for company. Now promise me!"

"Of course, you are my host, I promise I will not," said the priest, although he was rather bewildered. What could possibly happen in the middle of this dark night in the middle of this dark nowhere?

The old woman went out and the priest was left alone. The fire had died, and the only light in the hut was the dim lantern. For the first time he began to feel that he was in a strange, perhaps precarious place, and the old woman's words, "Sit where you are and do not go into the other room" aroused his curiosity and his fear.

What could be in that room that she did not wish him to see? He thought that the old woman would be angry with him if he broke his promise and so he stayed in his place by the fireside, but the minutes went slowly by and the old woman did not return. The young priest felt more and more frightened. What dreadful secret was in the room behind him? At last he could resist no longer. He got up and moved slowly toward the other room.

"She will not know that I have broken my promise unless I tell her. I will just take a look before she comes back," he said to himself.

He crept toward the forbidden spot. With trembling hands he slid the screen open. What he saw stopped the breath in his chest. In one corner skull upon skull rose in a pile to the ceiling, in another corner a heap of arm bones, in another a jumble of leg bones. The room was full of dead men's bones. The walls were splashed and the floor was covered with dead men's blood. The sickening smell drove him backwards into a heap of fright on the floor. His teeth chattered, and he could hardly crawl away from the dreadful spot.

"Merciful heaven!" he cried out. "What awful place have I come to? This kindly old woman is a yokai! May heaven help me or I am lost!"

With these words his wits came back to him and, snatching up his hat and staff, he rushed out of the house as fast as his legs could carry him. Out into the night he ran, his one thought to get as far as he could from the ghastly place. He had not gone far when he heard steps behind him and a voice crying, "Stop! Stop!"

He ran on, and as he ran he heard the steps behind him come nearer and nearer. He recognized the old woman's voice, which grew louder as she drew closer.

"Stop! Stop! Deceitful man, why did you look into the room?"

The priest forgot how tired he was and his feet flew over the ground. Fear gave him strength, for he knew that if the old woman caught him his skull would lie atop the pile in that terrible room. With all his heart he prayed for deliverance.

"Stop! Stop! You broke your promise, you must pay!"

The dreadful old hag rushed after him, her wild hair flying in the wind. Her rage changed her from a kindly old woman into the cannibal demon that she truly was. Yokai! In her hand she carried a wicked blood-stained knife, and she shrieked after him, "Stop! Stop!"

The young priest could see the houses of a distant town on the edge of the plain, but he knew he would never reach them in time. He could feel his legs failing him. He stumbled and fell. He dared not look behind him, but he felt the fetid breath of the demon upon his neck as she raised the bloody knife. Somewhere in the distance a rooster crowed. The dawn broke, and the darkness—and the yokai—vanished under the rising sun. The young priest pulled himself to his knees and thanked heaven for his deliverance.

He stumbled into the town and told his tale; in return, the townsfolk told him the story of the haunted plain. The young priest had never believed the stories that old women told around the braziers, that young girls told around the wells. But he had met the Demon Goblin of Adachigahara, and now he knew better.

——— To Your Good Health! ———

Ages 9–12. Retold by Janice M. Del Negro from *The Crimson Fairy Book* by Andrew Lang (Longmans, Green, 1903). Lang gave the *Russische Märchen* as his source for this tale, and Virginia Haviland includes it in her *Favorite Fairy Tales Told in Russia* (Little, Brown, 1961).

The humor of this tale depends on a sense of the absurd, so contrast between the assumed importance of the Tsar and the not-easily-impressed demeanor of the hero is key. Earlier versions of this tale have the shepherd surviving because he can stare like nobody's business, but the Tsarevna gets a slightly more important role in this retelling.

Long ago in Russia there lived a Tsar. When he was young he was a great soldier, brave and deadly, who bent men easily to his will. Now he was not so young and not so deadly, but he still bent men to his will for he was, after all, the Tsar. He decreed that whenever he sneezed everyone in the whole country had to say "To your good health!" Every single person, from babbling babies to old men, every single one, said it. For not to say it, well, the penalty was death and who wouldn't say "To your good health!" to avoid that?

Except . . . there was one person who would not say it.

Misha was a shepherd with eyes so bright they were sharp as ice. He had quite a stare that one, along with a strong will of his own. Misha, despite the royal decree, did not pay the Tsar's sneezes any mind.

The Tsar heard of this shepherd because, of course, the Tsar heard everything. He was very angry and sent for the shepherd to appear before him.

Misha came and stood before the Tsar, and stared at him with his bright, sharp eyes. The Tsar looked very grand and powerful, but however grand or powerful the Tsar might be, Misha was wholly unimpressed.

"I command you to say at once 'To my good health!'" shouted the Tsar.

"Immediately, sir," said Misha. "To my good health!"

"No, no, not to yours," roared the Tsar. "To mine, to mine, you rascal!"

"To mine, to mine, your Majesty," was Misha's answer.

"No, no, no, to mine, to my own," bellowed the Tsar, and beat on his chest in a rage.

"Well, yes, of course to mine, to my own," said Misha, and gently tapped his own chest.

The Tsar was beside himself with fury and did not know what to do, when the Imperial Chancellor whispered urgently in the shepherd's ear, "Say at once, say this very moment, 'To your good health, your Majesty,' for if you do not say it you will lose more than your sheep."

Now, the Tsarevna was sitting on a throne beside the Tsar, her father, and she looked as sweet and lovely as a golden dove. Misha's bright eyes laughed into her dark ones, and out of the air he pulled a thought.

"No, I will not say 'To your good health!' till I get the Tsarevna for my wife," he said.

When the Tsarevna heard what Misha said she could not help laughing, for there is no denying the fact that this young shepherd with the bright eyes pleased her very much: he was daring, he was brave, if a little foolish, and his eyes, well, his eyes told her things no other man's eyes had ever told her before.

But the Tsar was not as pleased as his daughter.

"Guards! Guards! Take this shepherd and throw him into the pit of the white bear!" The Tsarevna slipped quickly from the room.

"Now we'll see what you have to say," the Tsar gloated. "This white bear has not eaten for days and he will tear you limb from leg!"

The guards led Misha away and thrust him into the pit with the white bear, which had not eaten . . . until just now, when the Tsarevna secretly fed it. But a white bear is a fierce bear, and the door of the pit was hardly closed when the bear rushed at the shepherd. Misha turned his bright, sharp eyes on the bear, to look his death in the face. But Misha's bright eyes glowed strangely in the light of the pit, and when the bear saw those eyes it was so frightened that it sucked its own paws from sheer nervousness. Misha felt that if he once took his eyes off the beast he was a dead man, and in order to keep himself awake he made up songs and sang them, and so lulled the bear to sleep, charmed the listening Tsarevna, and passed the night away.

The next morning the Imperial Chancellor came to see Misha's bones and was amazed to find the shepherd alive and well. The chancellor took Misha to the Tsar.

"Well?" said the Tsar. "You have learned what it is to be very near death. Now will you say 'To my good health'?"

"I am not afraid of ten deaths!" Misha answered. "I will only say it if I may have the Tsarevna for my wife."

"Then go to your death," cried the Tsar. "Guards! Throw this dastard into the den with the wild boars." The Tsarevna slipped from the room.

The wild boars had not been fed for a week . . . unless you count just now, when the Tsarevna secretly fed them. Still, wild boars are fierce beasts, and when Misha was thrust into the den they rushed at him to tear him to pieces. But the shepherd took a little flute out of the sleeve of his jacket and began to play a merry tune. The wild boars got up on their hind legs and danced about the den. Misha would have given anything to be able to laugh, the boars looked so funny, but he dared not stop playing, for he knew the moment he stopped playing they would tear him to pieces. Misha played faster and faster till the boars tripped over each other and fell in a heap, exhausted from the dance.

Then the shepherd ventured to laugh at last, and he laughed so long and so loud he did not hear the hiding Tsarevna laughing along with him. When the Imperial Chancellor came early in the morning expecting to find the shepherd's bones, the tears of laughter were still running down Misha's cheeks.

As soon as the Tsar was dressed the shepherd was again brought before him.

"Well, you have learned what it feels to be near ten deaths. Now say 'To your good health!'"

"I do not fear a hundred deaths," said Misha, "and I will only say it if I may have the Tsarevna for my wife."

"Then go to a hundred deaths!" roared the Tsar, and he ordered the shepherd to be thrown down the well of scythes. The Tsarevna slipped from the room.

The guards dragged Misha away to a dark dungeon, in the middle of which was a deep well with sharp scythes all round from bottom to top. At the bottom of the well was a little light by which one could see if anything—or anyone—thrown in had fallen to the bottom.

Misha begged the guards to leave him alone a little while that he might look down into the well of scythes; perhaps he might make up his mind to say "To your good health" to the Tsar. So the guards gave the shepherd a moment alone to consider his fate. Misha was wondering how he was going to escape when a perfumed figure in a dark cloak stepped from a hidden passage, carrying what looked like a body.

"Here," the figure whispered. "Here is a bolster with a cape and a hat. Throw this down the well!" Misha's wits were as sharp as his eyes, and he was not one to waste time.

"I will never say it!" he howled at the top of his lungs. "I leap to my death my own man!"

Misha tossed the pillow dressed in the cloak into the well of scythes, and ducked back into the shadows of the hidden passage. The guards rushed in and peered into the well. All they could see was a dark figure in cloak and hat that blocked the light at the bottom. They returned to their quarters feeling, with some regret, that now that really was an end to the shepherd. But Misha hid in the shadows, laughing in the dark.

Quite early the next morning came the Imperial Chancellor, carrying a lamp to confirm the death of the willful shepherd. The Chancellor nearly fell backwards with surprise when he saw Misha alive and well. He brought him to the Tsar, whose fury was greater than ever.

"Well, now you have been near a hundred deaths; will you say 'To your good health'?"

Misha smiled at the Tsarevna and gave the same answer:

"I won't say it till the Tsarevna is my wife."

The Tsar decided if threats and violence would not work, he would try bribery.

"Perhaps after all you may do it for less," said the Tsar, and he ordered the state coach to carry himself and the shepherd to the silver wood. Amongst the sparkling silver leaves the silver blossoms perfumed the air.

"Do you see this silver wood?" asked the Tsar. "If you will say 'To your good health,' I will make it yours."

The sweet scent of the silver wood turned the shepherd hot and cold by turns, but he remembered the scent of the figure in the dark cloak and he said:

"I will not say it till the Tsarevna is my wife."

The Tsar was much vexed; he drove farther on till they came to a splendid castle, all of gold.

"Do you see this golden castle?" asked the Tsar. "I will give you the silver wood and the golden castle, if only you will say to me 'To your good health.'"

Misha had never seen stone that shone this bright, but he remembered the bright glint of the Tsarevna's smile and still he said:

"No, I will not say it till I have the Tsarevna for my wife."

The Tsar gave orders to drive on to the diamond pond, and there he tried once more.

"Do you see this diamond pond? I will give you the silver wood, the golden castle, and the diamond pond. All will be yours if you will but say 'To your good health!'"

The shepherd's eyes were dazzled by the brilliant pond, but the Tsarevna's eyes were more dazzling still.

"No, no; I will not say it till I have the Tsarevna for my wife."

Then the Tsar saw that all his efforts were useless and that he might as well give in.

"Fine! I will give you my daughter to wife; but, then, you really and truly must say to me, 'To your good health.'"

"Of course I'll say it," said Misha. "Why should I not say it? It stands to reason that I shall say it then."

At this the Tsar was more delighted than anyone could have believed. He made it known all through the country that there were to be great rejoicings, as the Tsarevna was going to be married. The people rejoiced to think that the Tsarevna, who had refused so many royal suitors, should end by falling in love with the bright-eyed shepherd.

Then there was such a wedding as had never been seen. Everyone ate and drank and danced. Even tiny newborn children had presents given them.

The greatest celebration was in the Tsar's palace. There the best bands played and the best food was cooked. Crowds of people sat down to table, and all was glee and merrymaking.

The highlight of the feast was when the great boar's head was brought in on a great platter and placed before the Tsar. The savory smell was so strong that the Tsar began to sneeze with all his might.

Misha leapt to his feet. "To your very good health!" he cried, before anyone else. The Tsar was so delighted that he did not regret having married his daughter to the shepherd.

In time, when the old Tsar died, Misha and the Tsarevna became Tsar and Tsarina. Misha made a very good tsar and never expected his people to wish him well against their wills. All the same, everyone did wish him well, for they all loved the shepherd with the bright, shining eyes.

CHAPTER 5

INTENSITY AND HONOR

Ages 12 to 14

Storytelling may appear too quaint and childish a pastime for young people ages 12 to 14 accustomed to sophisticated technology and instant access to digital recreation. Although contemporary adolescents have a veneer of sophistication that may seem daunting, they are just as susceptible to and appreciative of a well-told tale as any other listener. The elements of a successful tale for this age group include a strong pace, forward momentum, interesting characters, high stakes (life, love, fortune), and a satisfying conclusion. Some storytellers find this age a challenge, but young teens are an excellent listening audience if you keep certain things in mind.

Do not set yourself up for failure by being cute. Cute is the kiss of death with this age group. Once adolescence begins, youth want desperately to identify with their older peers. They are uninterested in anything that ties them to what they consider childish things; efforts at participatory stories or sing-alongs will, for the most part, be met with stony, judgmental silence. Selection, always important, is crucial with this age group, because the narrative must be strong enough to carry the listeners, no matter how reluctant, suspicious, or just plain uninformed they may be.

Adolescents 12 to 14 years old are a whirlpool of emotional intensity, constantly shifting and changing, easily triggered. Stories selected must recognize—and match—the emotional complexity of this developmental stage, but the emotions within the tale itself must be handled with total control: language, pace, and structure are critical. Parallels can be drawn with poetry; just as poetic form disciplines intense emotions, the structural form of oral narrative contains the emotional content of the story, no matter how strong.

Unlike preschoolers and primary graders who are always willing to play, those 12 to 14 years old are trying to put aside childish things, and that includes anything reminiscent of playing. Telling to this age group requires a confident, controlled presentation. First, though, you have to get them to listen to you. Adolescents—really, any listeners who have not experienced storytelling—often have mistaken perceptions about storytelling. They associate it with reading aloud, from books, to the very young. A good way to catch the attention of these listeners is to spook them with a gory, supernatural tale that is obviously not for children. Once they have had a positive experience with storytelling, their preconceptions fall away, and they will willingly listen to any other stories you want to tell them.

Some storytellers are surprised to discover that young teens greatly appreciate lushly romantic tales in which characters find destined love, overcome obstacles, journey into danger, and outwit fate. Adolescents may groan at the idea of hearing a romantic story, but don't let that stop you. Romantic and quest tales, with magical and mysterious elements, hold a great deal of appeal. Stories such as "East o' the Sun and West o' the Moon," "The Princess on the Glass Hill," and "Vasilisa the Beautiful" all have strong plots and imagery that work well when telling to this age.

Early adolescents are moving from a literal interpretation of the world to an understanding of more abstract concepts such as justice, honor, and perseverance. They are beginning to think abstractly, and, believe it or not, they can recognize the potential consequences of thoughts and actions. They are often introspective, empathetic, and very aware of social constructs and constraints. Through storytelling, these listeners can vicariously experience dangerous events and intense emotions without actually having to participate in them. Critical for this age is the idea of overcoming obstacles, such as in "The Hunter and the Doves" from the Panchatantra, a collection of fables from India. A bevy of doves caught beneath a hunter's net unite to escape; the doves grip the net in their beaks and fly together, thus freeing them all. The right story can impart an understanding that taking action can change a life, alter circumstances, and alleviate suffering. Storytelling is a way of giving this extremely vulnerable age group a sense that they can be the heroes of their own lives and the creators of their own stories.

Loyalty and friendship are paramount for 12- to 14-year-olds; they are moving away from their parents or guardians and closer to their peers. They are often emotionally vulnerable and have a tendency to overreact to perceived slights, rejection, and embarrassment. Listeners at this stage are looking for character models, for reasons for being, for their own identities. The stories you select to tell to this age group should provide them with heroes and heroines worth their time, with feelings that match the intensity of their own. Look for stories with big emotions, big crises, big conflicts, and big payoffs. Of course, the stories always have to be entertaining.

Humor is welcome, but the humor has to be built into the plot, through the actions and dialogue of the characters. Stories that point out the foibles of the foolish, the pompous, or the arrogant have a great deal of appeal as these listeners struggle to find their own way outside school or family. Both serious and humorous tales of hubristic authority (and its subsequent downfall) will catch the imagination of these listeners. Irreverent tales also work well, such as the Jewish folktale "The Price of Smells" or the Grimm folktale "Clever Grethel" (retold later in this chapter).

Younger listeners are willing to participate in the telling of the story in an obvious way, but the participation of 12- to 14-year-olds is less overt. This age group requires subtlety and sophistication in both form and content; know your story and deliver it with friendly authority. This is a good age for epics, myths, even narrative ballads. Norse and Greek myths ("How Thor Lost His Hammer," "Cupid and Psyche"), longer quest-oriented folktales, adventures, and, yes, the occasional romantic folktale, happy or tragic ("The Crane Wife") all work. The enormous surge in popularity of retellings of traditional folk and fairy tales in contemporary media is a boon for storytellers working with listeners 12 to 14 years old; traditional tales combined with contemporary reimaginings that offer a twist on the well-known have strong appeal for this and older ages.

Successful storytelling to this age is built on the confidence the teller has in the tale, so selection is, as always, a priority. Straightforward, matter-of-fact presentation of the most outlandish details will support the authority of the teller and draw in the listener. The storyteller must present her or his folktales with authority backed by hundreds of years of telling success. If you doubt your own authority, remember the words of Laura S. Emerson: "Self-confidence is gained by preparation and practice" (*Storytelling, the Art and the Purpose*, Zondervan, 1959).

Presenting to this age requires control over both your story and its delivery. Language must be specific, concrete, and surprising; cliché is boring, not only for the listeners but also for the storyteller. Although cute and sentimental do not have great appeal here, this does not mean that admirable character traits and strong emotions are absent; on the contrary, they are critical elements in stories that appeal to these listeners.

Similarly, although melodrama works with younger listeners, adolescents must be wooed into the storytelling experience with clarity and forthrightness. If there is melodrama, the teller must present it to adolescent listeners as if they are in on the joke; at this age, being let in on adult secrets is a deeply held desire. Any indication that what you are telling is suitable for adults, that you see and treat your listeners with the respect due to maturity, will be well received. Stories with unexpected or surprise endings work well with this age. Consider a traditional Lemba tale from Africa, "Strength," in which a man brings a gun to a contest of strength among the animals. The gun results in death, not strength, and as a result man must always walk alone.

The surefire winner with adolescents, however, is the supernatural or gory story. These can be stories with actual supernatural elements such as ghosts, or gory tales about murder and mayhem. Discussion of the suitability of the supernatural tale is ongoing, the general conclusion being that the supernatural or gory tale allows listeners to experience strong emotions or perilous adventures without serious consequence. The fascination listeners of all ages have for these stories consistently surprises me; you will get a listening audience (of all ages) for ghost tales when you cannot get a listening audience for any other type of storytelling event. As previously stated, be clear about the content of your program and the suitable age for attendees in any promotion, and then reiterate the content and the recommended age of attendees before the program begins. The decision to stay and listen belongs to the listener, or, in the case of the younger listener, to the parent or caregiver. School librarians and teachers telling these tales in their classrooms are the best judges of what their community finds acceptable. My opinion here is that the listener of spooky stories, unlike the viewer of gory movies, only takes the images in the tales as far as is comfortable; film or other concrete images do not allow for that individual control. Always remember who your listeners are: the gory tale that is acceptable for 12- to 14-year-olds is not necessarily acceptable for 9- to 12-year-olds. Consider content and impact: how do you want your listeners to feel after the story (or the program) is over?

Sources for supernatural or gory tales abound: a large number of such tales are included in general folktale collections as well as collections themed toward this type of tale. Think of these tales as the original virtual experience. Adolescents find the spooky or suspenseful tale intriguing on a number of levels, one being that spooky stories are definitely not for little children. Hence, those 12 to 14 years old are more willing to enter the story experience because the scary story is obviously more adult than childish. My favorites for capturing the desperately cool 12- to 14-year-old audience are "Mary Culhane and the Dead Man," in Molly Bang's *Goblin's Giggle*, or "Mr. Fox," found in Joseph Jacobs's *English Fairy Tales* and in the following StoryCoaching section.

STORYCOACHING

"Mr. Fox," retold by Janice M. Del Negro from *English Fairy Tales* by Joseph Jacobs (David Nutt, 1890).

"Mr. Fox" is a very old tale, mentioned by Shakespeare in Much Ado about Nothing. *The tale is a Bluebeard variant, which is a variant of the*

Grimm "Robber Bridegroom" story. Suffice it to say there is nothing new under the sun—this story could be from today's headlines. The gory details of this tale are controlled by the structure of the tale and repetition of the refrain, which not only control the potential sensational nature of the tale but build the suspense inexorably.

Lady Mary was young, and Lady Mary was fair. She had two brothers and more suitors than she could count. But of them all, the handsomest and most dashing was Mr. Fox, whom she met when she was down at her father's country house.

The strong structure and rhythmic language of this tale begin immediately, with the repetition of "Lady Mary" and the pairing of the adjectives describing Mr. Fox. Open with a commanding tone, as if introducing a great drama—which you are.

No one knew who Mr. Fox was; but he was certainly brave, and surely rich, and of all her suitors Lady Mary cared for him alone. At last it was agreed upon between them that they should be married. Lady Mary asked Mr. Fox where they should live, and he described to her his castle, and where it was; but, strange to say, he did not ask her, or her brothers, to come and see it.

Speak slowly and thoughtfully on the phrase "No one knew who Mr. Fox was" and pick up the pace with "but he was certainly brave, and surely rich" as if to indicate the former does not matter because of the latter.

So one day, near the wedding day, when her brothers were out, and Mr. Fox—he said—was away for a day or two on business, Lady Mary set out for Mr. Fox's castle.

The pause is an effective attention-getting tool, emphasizing anything that comes before or after it. Pause briefly before and after "he said" in the phrase "and Mr. Fox—he said—was away for a day or two on business."

After much searching she came at last to Mr. Fox's castle, and a fine strong place it was, with high walls and a deep moat. When she came up to the gate, she saw written on it in words of iron, "Be bold, be bold."

Point to the words on the gate, perhaps sketching with your hand an arc in the air above your head to indicate the height of the gate and the shape of the words. Pause briefly after the phrase "Be bold, be bold."

Oh, but Lady Mary was a brave soul, she was. As the gate was open, she went through it, and found no one there. So she went up to the front door, and over it she found written in words of wood, "Be bold, be bold. But not too bold."

Slow down the delivery here, and speak quietly. A slight drop in volume will cause listeners to lean forward to hear better. Again, indicate the height of the door and the shape of the words. Pause briefly after the phrase "Be bold, be bold," then continue "But not too bold," giving a short beat between the words to emphasize the rhythm of the phrase.

Oh, but Lady Mary was a brave soul, she was. She opened the door, but found no one. Still she went on into the house, till she found a great stairway. She went up the broad stairs till she came to a door at the end of the hall, over which was written in words of red, "Be bold, be bold. But not too bold, lest your heart's blood run cold."

Oh, but Lady Mary was a brave soul, she was, she was, and she opened the door, and she saw, oh, what she saw . . .

Pause, as if you can't bear to say it, and then whisper:

. . . why, bodies and bones, bodies and bones of young women, all, all the bodies and bones, all stained with blood.

This should be delivered in a hoarse whisper, keeping the rhythm of the language strong and clear.

Oh, but Lady Mary was a brave soul, she was, but she thought it was high time to get out of that horrid place, and she closed the door, went through the hall, and was just going down the stairs, when who should she see through the window?

Pick up the pace here, to keep pace with Mary running from the room. On "who should she see through the window?" pick up the volume somewhat as well to indicate panic.

It was him!

Whisper this. The contrast between the higher and lower volumes will pull listeners closer.

It was Mr. Fox, dragging a young woman from the gateway to the door. Lady Mary raced down the stairs, and hid herself behind a huge cask, a wooden barrel that sat beneath the stairway.

If you are using language that may be unfamiliar to your listeners, explain that language in the context of the tale instead of having a vocabulary lesson before you begin the story.

And just in time, for Mr. Fox came in with the poor young woman who, mercy of mercies, had fainted dead away.

Terror and panic should be indicated by a rushed delivery.

Just as he passed where Lady Mary crouched hidden, Mr. Fox saw a ruby ring glittering on the finger of the young woman he dragged. He tried to pull it off, but it was tightly fixed, so Mr. Fox cursed and swore, and drew his sword and cut off the young woman's hand. The hand flew, ring and all, into the air, and fell, of all places in the world to fall, into Lady Mary's lap. Mr. Fox did not waste time searching, but dragged the young lady upstairs into the bloody chamber.

Slow down on the final words here; pause briefly, and pick up the pace as Lady Mary starts running.

As soon as she heard the door close on that bloody room, Lady Mary crept out of the house, through the gateway, and ran as fast as she could, carrying that bloody hand all the way home.

Significant pause here.

Now it happened that the very next day the marriage contract of Lady Mary and Mr. Fox was to be signed, and there was a splendid breakfast before that. Mr. Fox, seated at the table opposite Lady Mary, said, "How pale you are this morning, my dear."

This should be said very matter-of-factly to contrast with the scene of carnage just escaped. Mr. Fox speaking to Lady Mary should be all sweetness and concern.

"Yes," said Lady Mary. "Last night I had terrible dreams."

Speak slowly and softly, but firmly. Lady Mary knows she has him, she knows what he has done, and she is not afraid.

"Dreams?" said Mr. Fox. "Tell me your dreams, and, once spoken, all terrors will fade in the light of day."

Mr. Fox, on the other hand, does not know what is about to happen. He is confident, avuncular.

"I dreamed," said Lady Mary, "that I found your castle in the woods, with high walls, and a deep moat, and over the gateway was written in words of iron, 'Be bold, be bold.'"

Pause here as Lady Mary reveals this and looks to see how Mr. Fox takes it.

"But it was not so," said Mr. Fox. "And it is not so."

Speak slowly and thoughtfully. Here is the first moment of hesitation, the first time Mr. Fox is unsure.

"In my dream it was so. In my dream I came to the front door and over it was written in words of wood, 'Be bold, be bold. But not too bold.'"

Lady Mary is gaining confidence; her delivery here is direct, almost confrontational.

"But it was not so," said Mr. Fox. "And it is not so."

Forcefully, as if Mr. Fox is trying to insist, as if by saying so he makes it so.

"In my dream it was so. In my dream I went upstairs, and at the end of a hallway there was a door, and over it was written in words of red, 'Be bold, be bold. But not too bold, lest your heart's blood run cold.'"

Softly and relentlessly.

"But it was not so," said Mr. Fox. "And it is not so."

Blustering, and losing ground.

"And then—and then I opened the door, and what I saw, oh, what I saw . . ."

Pause, as if you can't bear to say it, and then whisper:

"The room was filled with bodies and bones, bodies and bones of young women, all, all bodies and bones, all stained with blood."

Softly and relentlessly.

"But it was not so," said Mr. Fox. "And it is not so."

Pick up the pace and volume here to indicate Mr. Fox's rising panic.

"I rushed down the stairs, and then I saw you, Mr. Fox, coming up to the front door, dragging after you a poor young woman by the arm. I hid myself and held my breath. As you passed me, Mr. Fox, you tried to get off her ruby ring, and when you could not, you drew out your sword and hacked off her hand."

Said matter-of-factly and distinctly.

"It was not so, and it is not so, and God forbid it should be so," said Mr. Fox, and he rose from his seat.

Said quickly, panicked and angry.

Lady Mary cried out, "But it was so, and it is so, and here's hand and ring to prove it so." And from the folds of her dress Lady Mary pulled that woman's hand and pointed it straight at Mr. Fox.

She is the avenger; her tone should be confident and merciless.

He did not even have a moment to pray to his God before Lady Mary's brothers and the breakfast guests fell on Mr. Fox with their swords and cut him into a thousand pieces.

Speak rhythmically and clearly. Keep the conclusion abrupt yet clean. Do not be surprised if there is a moment of silence at the end of the tale.

Tales-to-Text

Bodkin, Odds. *The Crane Wife*. Illus. by Gennady Spirin. Sandpiper, 2002.

"Cupid and Psyche." *Greek Myths* by Olivia E. Coolidge. Houghton Mifflin, 1949.

Dembicki, Matt, ed. *Trickster: Native American Tales, a Graphic Collection*. Fulcrum Books, 2010.

"The Fire on the Mountain." *The Fire on the Mountain and Other Stories from Ethiopia and Eritrea*. Retold by Harold Courlander and Wolf Leslau. Henry Holt, 1995. See also the picture book by Jane Kurtz, *Fire on the Mountain*, illus. by E. B. Lewis (Simon and Schuster, 1994).

"Godfather Death." *Grimms' Tales for Young and Old: The Complete Stories*. Trans. by Ralph Manheim. Anchor, 1983.

Hale, Shannon. *Calamity Jack*. Bloomsbury, 2010.

———. *Rapunzel's Revenge*. Bloomsbury, 2008.

Holt, David, and Bill Mooney, eds. *The Exploding Toilet: Modern Urban Legends*. August House, 2004.

———. *Spiders in the Hairdo: Modern Urban Legends*. August House, 1999.

"Keewahkee." *When the Chenoo Howls: Native American Tales of Terror*. Retold by Joseph and James Bruchac. Illus. by William Sauts Netamuâxwe Bock. Walker, 1998.

Kimmel, Eric A. *Sword of the Samurai: Adventure Stories from Japan*. Harcourt, 1999.

"La Muerta: Godmother Death." *Ready-to-Tell Tales*. Ed. by David Holt and Bill Mooney. August House, 1994.

Marcantonio, Patricia Santos. *Red Ridin' in the Hood and Other Cuentos*. Farrar, Straus and Giroux, 2005.

"Mary Culhane and the Dead Man." *Goblin's Giggles and Other Stories*. Retold by Molly Bang. Peter Smith, 1988.

McCaughrean, Geraldine. *Gilgamesh the Hero*. Eerdmans Books for Young Readers, 2003.

"Nesoowa and the Chenoo." *The Serpent Slayer and Other Stories of Strong Women*. Retold by Katrin Tchana. Illus. by Trina Schart Hyman. Little, Brown, 2000.

"Pygmalion and Galatea." *Mythology*. Retold by Edith Hamilton. Back Bay, 1998.

"The Sea Captain's Wife." *Twelve Great Black Cats and Other Eerie Scottish Tales*. Retold by Sorche Nic Leodhas. Dutton, 1971.

Sheinkin, Steve. *Rabbi Harvey vs. the Wisdom Kid: A Graphic Novel of Dueling Jewish Folktales in the Wild West*. Jewish Lights, 2010.

"Strength." *Peace Tales*. Retold by Margaret Read MacDonald. August House, 2006.

Tarnowska, Wafa. *The Arabian Nights*. Illus. by Carole Henaff. Barefoot Books, 2010.

"The Three Young Men and Death." *Medieval Tales*. Retold by Jennifer Westwood. Coward-McCann, 1968.

Valentino, Jim, and Kristin K. Simon, eds. *Fractured Fables*. Image Comics, 2010.

Vande Velde, Vivian. *Cloaked in Red*. Marshall Cavendish, 2010.

STORIES

for Ages 12 to 14

A Ghost Story

Ages 12–14. Adapted for telling by Janice M. Del Negro from *Nights with Uncle Remus: Myths and Legends of the Old Plantation* by Joel Chandler Harris (Houghton, Mifflin, 1883). An abbreviated version of this story is also available in *More Scary Stories to Tell in the Dark* by Alvin Schwartz (Lippincott, 1984) under the title "Clinkety-Clink."

In the Harris version of this story, the wind says "Buzz-zoo-o-o-o-o!" but I prefer the whispering moan of "Shhhhoooooooh." You decide what wind sound is both the most comfortable for you and the spookiest for your listeners. This is a story that should be related as if it were gossip. Volume and pace are key in the telling of scary tales, so take your time and remember that a whisper is often scarier than a shout. It is possible to turn this into a jump tale depending on how you time the conclusion.

Once there was an old woman and a younger man. They were neighbors. Not good neighbors, but neighbors. Anyway, they lived close to one another. The old woman, she just went about her business. And the man? Well, he didn't have enough to do because he paid way too much attention to that woman's business instead of his own.

The old woman, though, she tended to her own business so much that she took sick and died. The man, minding the old woman's business instead of his own, told her folks she was dead, and her folks came and laid her out. They lit some candles and they sat up through the night with her body, and they put two big round shiny silver dollars on her eyes to hold her eyelids down.

Those silver dollars looked mighty pretty. They were all the money the old woman had, and her folks put them on her eyelids to hold them down. After they had done all that was proper and right, the folks called on the neighbor man, the one that wouldn't mind his own business. They asked him would he dig the grave to bury the woman. When he said yes, the old woman's folks went off to tend to the business of the living.

Well, the man tended to the dead woman's business one more time. He dug the grave and made ready to bury her, all right and proper. He looked at the silver dollars shining on the dead woman's eyelids, holding them closed. Those silver dollars shone mighty pretty. The man took those silver dollars off the dead woman's eyes and weighed them in his hand. Those coins felt mighty good, but when the man looked at the woman he saw her eyes open. She was looking right at him, and he took those coins and put them back right where he got them.

Well, then the man, he got a wagon and he laid the woman in the bottom and hauled her out to the burying ground. When he got there he did all the right things—he put her gently in the ground, he even said a prayer—but when he turned to pick up the shovel to fill in the grave, the light flashed on those shiny silver dollars holding the old woman's eyelids down. He should have minded his own business then, but he didn't. He grabbed those silver coins off the old woman's eyes, grabbed the shovel, and filled up the grave quicker than water.

When he got home he put those heavy silver coins in a tin box and shook it. Clinkety-clink! Clinkety-clink! Those coins rattled loud and those coins rattled nice. Clinkety-clink! "Good," thought the man. The man didn't feel so good though. He knew. He just knew the dead woman's eyelids were stretched wide open looking for him. He shook the tin box. Clinkety-clink! Those coins rattled loud and those coins rattled nice.

Well, the man put those coins in the tin box on the mantel shelf, over the fireplace. The day went down slow, the night came up fast. The wind began to rise. The wind whistled high, the wind whispered low. The wind blew on top of the house, under the house, all around the house. The man sat by the fire and listened. The wind said, "Shhhhh-oooooh!" The man listened. The wind wept and cried. The wind blew on top of the house, under the house, all around the house. The wind found the cracks in the walls and blew into the house. "Shhhhh-oooooh! Ooooooh!"

The man felt strange. He listened and listened to the wind, but by and by he got too tired to be scared of a windy night and he went to bed. He flung a fresh knot into the fire, jumped into bed, curled himself up, and put his head under the covers.

The wind whispered and cried. The wind hunted for cracks. "Shhhhh-oooooh!" The man kept his head under the covers. The lighted knot flickered and flared. The man didn't dare to move. The wind hunted for cracks, blew in and whistled. "Shhhhh-oooooh!" The lighted knot flickered and flared. The man stayed under the covers.

He shivered and shook like swamp fever. He scarcely dared to wink his eyes. While he was lying there shaking the wind was blowing, and the fire flickering. Clinkety-clink! He heard a different kind of noise. Clinkety-clink!

"Hey! Who is stealing my money?"

The man kept his head covered and listened. He heard the wind blow, and then . . . Clinkety-clink, clinkety-clink!

He flung off the covers and sat right up in bed. The fire flickered and flared, and the wind whispered and groaned. The man went and put a chain and a bar across the door. Then he went back to bed, and he had just put his head on the pillow when . . . Clink, clink, clinkety-clink! The man sat up and looked, but there was nothing at all.

Just about the time he was going to lie down again . . . Clinkety-clink. The sound came from the mantel shelf. Clinkety-clink. The sound came from the tin box on the mantel shelf. Clinkety-clink. The sound was the silver coins rattling in the tin box on the mantel shelf.

"It can't be," thought the man.

The man walked slowly to the mantel shelf and opened the tin box. The two coins rested side by side in the bottom of the box. He shut the box and set it down on the shelf. Clinkety-clinkety-clink.

The man opened the box and looked at the money. Those two silver dollars rested side by side in the bottom of the box. The wind whispered and cried. "Shhhhh-oooooh!" And something else, way off yonder, moaned, "Where's my money? Oh, give me my money!"

"It can't be!" said the man. "It can't!"

But it was, oh it was. Clinkety-clink.

"Where's my money? I want my money!"

Well, then the man was scared clear through. He ran and jumped into bed. Clinkety-clink. He pulled the covers over his head.

Something cried not so way off, "I want my money! Oh, give me my money!"

Clinkety-clink.

"It can't be," said the man. "It can't."

But it was.

The wind whispered and cried. "Shhhhh-oooooh!"

Something moaned a short way away, "I want my money! Oh, give me my money!"

Clinkety-clink.

The man shook worse and worse. The wind groaned and whispered. "Shhhhh-oooooh!"

Something moaned right close by, "Oh, give me my money!"

Clinkety-clink.

"It can't be," said the man.

The door swung open.

"It can't be," said the man.

The old woman he buried in the burying ground, she stood there, there in the doorway. Her eyes were open and wide, but cloudy-white with death. Clinkety-clink. The man was so scared he could only shake. The wind whistled through the cracks. "Shhhhh-oooooh!" The money rattled, clinkety-clink.

The old woman cried, "Oh, where's my money? Oh, give me my money!"

"It can't be!" said the man.

Clinkety-clink. The dead woman heard the money, but she couldn't see it, and she groped around, and groped around, and groped around with her hands in the air.

The wind whispered. "Shhhhh-oooooh!" The fire was flickering. The money was rattling. Clinkety-clink! The man was shaking and shivering. The dead woman was groping around and saying, "Give me my money! Oh, who's got my money?"

The wind blew. The tin box shook. Clinkety-clink! The dead woman groped and cried, until by and by she found him. She found the man, shaking in his bed. She reached out her hands, groping for the coins, groping for his throat, and hissed, "You've got my money!"

But he doesn't have it anymore.

—————————— **Clever Grethel** ——————————

Ages 12–14. Retold by Janice M. Del Negro from *Household Stories from the Collection of the Brothers Grimm*, translated by Lucy Crane (MacMillan, 1886).

Grethel is in many ways something of a trickster figure, although not in the traditional mold. She is smart, funny, and audacious, and she does exactly what she pleases, paying no attention to what other people think. She is bossy and sure of herself, but never so much that she is a bully; the listeners must always love her. She is, as the story says, cheeky, but always manages to come out on top.

There was once a cook called Grethel, who wore fancy shoes with bright red heels, and when she went out in them she thought herself very fine indeed. The neighbors thought something else altogether about Grethel, but she didn't care. She cheekily wore her shoes with red heels, and as she was such a good cook, what the neighbors thought went quite unmentioned.

When Grethel came home from her walks around town she would take a drink of cider to refresh herself while she was working, and as that gave her an appetite, she would nibble on some of the best of whatever she was cooking.

"A clever cook knows how things taste," said Grethel.

Now it happened that the master of the house, Grethel's employer, said to her, "Grethel, I have a dinner guest this evening; you must make ready a pair of roast chickens."

"Certainly, sir," answered Grethel, for she was a very clever cook who knew how to earn her money. So she killed the chickens, cleaned them, plucked them, and put them on the spit, and then, as the evening drew near, placed them before the fire to roast. First they began to brown, and then they were nearly done, but still the guest had not arrived.

"Some people just don't appreciate how much work goes into a good meal," said Grethel to her master. "If your guest does not make haste the chickens will be ruined. It's a pity and a shame not to eat them now, just when they are done to perfection."

The master said he would run himself and fetch the guest. As soon as he was gone, Grethel took the chickens from before the fire.

"Standing so long before the fire," said she, "makes one hot and thirsty, and who knows when they will come! Some people just don't appreciate how much work goes into a good meal. I will run down to the cellar and have a mug of cider."

So down she ran and took up a mug. "Here's to me!" she said and took a big gulp. "One good gulp deserves another," she said, so she took another. Then she went back up to the kitchen and put the chickens to the fire again. She turned the spit briskly round and basted those birds with butter. Those chickens began to smell so good that Grethel just could not help herself. She took the choicest piece, licked her fingers, and cried, "Well, I never! These chickens are so good; it's a sin and a shame that no one is here to eat them! Some people just don't appreciate how much work goes into a good meal."

So she ran to the window to see if her master and his guest were coming, but as she could see nobody she went back to her chickens. "Why, one of the wings is burning," she said. "I had better eat it and get it out of the way." So she cut it off and ate it up, and it tasted very good, and then she thought the chicken looked a little lopsided, so she said, "I had better cut off the other wing too." When both wings had been disposed of she went and looked for the master and his guest, but still they did not come.

"Who knows," said she, "whether they are coming or not? I may as well make myself happy. First I will have a good drink and then a good meal, and when all is done I shall be easy." So first she ran down into the cellar and had some cider, and then she ran back to the kitchen and ate up one whole chicken!

When that was done, Grethel looked for the master and his guest. Still they did not come, and Grethel eyed the other chicken. "What one is the other must be. It is only fair that they should be both treated alike; perhaps, when I have had another drink, I shall be able to manage it." So first she ran down into the cellar and had some cider, and then she ran back to the kitchen and the second chicken went the way of the first.

Just as she was finishing the last buttery bite, the master came back.

"Make haste, Grethel," cried he, "the guest is coming directly!"

"Right away, sir," Grethel answered. "Dinner will be on the table lickety-split!"

The master went into the dining room and, taking up the great carving knife with which he meant to carve the chickens, he sharpened it upon the step. Presently the guest arrived, knocking very politely at the front door. Grethel ran to the door, and when she opened it she put her finger on her lips saying, "Hush! Run away as fast as you can! My master asked you to supper, but he really means to cut off your ears! Just listen to how he is sharpening his knife!"

The guest, hearing the noise of the knife being sharpened, ran off as fast as he could, and Grethel ran to her master.

"A pretty guest you have asked to the house!" cried she.

"Why Grethel, what do you mean?" asked he.

"What indeed," said she. "Why, your guest has gone and run away with my pair of chickens that I spent all day roasting to perfection!"

"That's a greedy way to behave!" said the master, feeling very sorry about the chickens. "He might at least have left me one, for I am very hungry."

The master went to the door, and seeing his guest running away in the distance the master called out, "Stop!" But the guest kept running. So after the guest ran the master, the knife still in his hand, crying out, "Only one! At least let me have one!" meaning that the guest should let him have at least one of the chickens and not take both, but the guest thought the master meant to have only one of his ears instead of two, and so he ran that much faster.

That night the master went to bed hungry, but Grethel did not. The next day she wore her fancy shoes with the bright red heels all around the town, and as she was such a good cook, what the neighbors thought went quite unmentioned.

The Magic Pipe: A Norse Tale

Ages 12–14. Retold by Janice M. Del Negro from *Tales of Folk and Fairies* by Katharine Pyle (Little, Brown, 1919).

This is a long story but it has a good amount of dialogue to liven things up. Keep the pace moving fairly quickly, and don't forget to differentiate the deliveries of the repetitive elements—that is, make sure anything repeated is stated or delivered differently each time. Your listeners will be more engaged with the narrative if you surprise them with different language.

There were once three brothers, all the sons of the same father and mother. The two older brothers were hard-working but greedy, with no care except as to how they might better themselves in the world. But the youngest, whose name was Boots, was a dreamer, and he was quite content to sit in the chimney corner and warm his shins and think about things.

One day the eldest son came to his father and said, "I have it in mind to go to the King's castle and take service there, for I hear the King needs a man to herd his rabbits. The wages are six dollars a week, and if anyone can keep the herd together and bring all the rabbits safe home every night without losing one of them the King will give him the Princess for a wife."

The father thought that was something worth trying for, so the eldest son grabbed his hat and off he set for the palace. He had not gone far when he came to the edge of a forest, and there was an old crone with a green nose a yard long. That long, green nose was caught in a crack of a log, and the old crone was dancing and hopping about, but for all her dancing and hopping she got no farther than that one spot, for her nose held her there. The lad stopped and stared at her, and then he laughed and laughed till his sides ached.

"You gawk!" screamed the old hag. "Come and drive a wedge in the crack so I can get my nose out. Here I have stood for twice a hundred years, and no Christian soul has come to set me free."

"If you have stood there twice a hundred years you might as well stay a while longer. I'm expected at the King's palace, and I have no time to waste," said the eldest brother, and away he went, one foot before the other, leaving the old crone with her nose still in the crack.

When the eldest brother came to the palace, he knocked at the door. "I have come to herd the royal rabbits," he proclaimed. The guardsman brought the eldest son straight to the King.

"Oho, yes!" the King said. "Yes, I need someone to herd my rabbits. The wages are good, and there's a chance of winning the Princess to boot. But there is a third part of this bargain."

The King grinned.

"If you fail to keep the herd together, if you lose just one baby rabbit, you will get such a beating as will turn you black and blue."

"Sir, that is unpleasant," said the eldest brother. "But I am confident I will succeed."

"Very well then!" said the King. "Be off with you!"

So the eldest son was taken out to the rabbit paddock, and a pretty sight it was to see all those bunnies hopping and frisking about inside the fence, hundreds and hundreds of them, big and little.

All morning the rabbits were kept inside the fence, the eldest son watching, and all went well. The trouble came later, when the rabbits were let out on the hills for a run and a bite of fresh grass. The eldest son could no more keep those bunnies together than if they had been sparks from a fire. Away they sped, some one way and some another, into the woods and over the hills—there was no keeping track of them. The eldest son shouted and ran and ran and shouted till the sweat poured down his face, but he could not herd those rabbits. By the time evening came he had scarce a score of them to drive home to the palace.

There on the palace steps stood the King with a stout rod in his hands, all ready to give the eldest son a beating. And a beating it was, I can tell you. When the King had finished with the eldest son he could hardly stand. Home he went, with only his sore bones for pay.

Then it was the second brother's turn. He went to his father and said, "I have it in mind to go to the King's castle, for I hear the King needs someone to herd his rabbits. If anyone can bring those rabbits home every night without losing one bunny the King will give him the Princess for a wife."

The father thought that was something anyway, so the second son grabbed his hat and off he set on the same road as his brother. After a while he came to the place where the old crone was dancing about with her long, green nose still caught in the crack of a log. The second son stood for a while and laughed and laughed till the tears ran down his cheeks. The old hag was raging.

"You gawk!" she cried. "Come and drive a wedge in the crack so I can get my nose out! Here I have stood for twice a hundred years, and no Christian soul has come to set me free."

"If you have been there that long it will not hurt to stay a bit longer," said the youth. "I'm on my way to the King's palace to win a Princess for a wife and have no time for you." And away he went, leaving the old woman screaming after him.

When the second brother came to the palace, he knocked at the door. "I have come to herd the royal rabbits," he proclaimed. The guardsman brought the second son straight to the King.

"Oho, yes!" the King said. "Yes, I still need someone to herd my rabbits. The wages are good, and there's a chance of winning the Princess. But . . ." and the King grinned. "If you fail to keep the herd together, if you lose just one baby rabbit, you will get such a beating as will turn you black and blue."

"Sir, that is unpleasant," said the second brother. "But I am confident I will succeed where my older brother failed."

"Very well then!" said the King. "Be off with you!"

So the second son was taken out to the rabbit paddock. There they were, hundreds of bunnies hopping about, big and little.

That morning all went well, but as soon as the gate opened in the fence, well, what happened that day happened this day, and when the King finished with the second brother he was black and blue from head to heels, and that is all he got for all his trying.

Now after the second brother had come home with bumps and bruises, Boots sat and thought and sat and thought about what had happened. After a while he stood up and shook the ashes from his clothes.

"Now it's my turn to try and win the Princess for my wife," Boots announced.

His brothers scoffed and hooted.

"You're a fool," said one.

"A dreamer," said the other. "How can you succeed where we have failed?"

"Well, fool or dreamer or something else," smiled Boots. "At any rate I will take my chances."

So off he went, just as his two brothers had before him. After a while he came to the very same road and the very same crone, her long, green nose caught in the very same crack in the very same log. He stood and stared and stared, for it was a curious sight.

"Oh, you gawk! Why do you stand there staring?" cried the old hag. "Here I have been for twice a hundred years, and no Christian soul will take the trouble to set me free. Drive a wedge into the crack so that I may get my nose out."

"That I will and gladly, good mother," said Boots. "Two hundred years is a long time to have one's nose pinched in a crack."

Quickly he found a wedge and drove it into the crack with a stone. The old hag pulled her nose out and gave Boots a good long look. She liked what she saw.

"Now you have done me a good turn, and I have it in mind to do the same for you," she said. With that she took a pipe, a pretty little whistle, out of the pocket of her skirt.

"You take this," she said. "This pipe will come in handy if you're on your way to the King's palace. If you blow on the right end of the whistle the things around you will be blown every which way as if a strong wind had struck them. If you blow on the wrong end those things will be gathered together again. And those are not the only tricks the pipe has, for if any one takes it from you, you have only to wish for it to have it back in your hand again."

"Well, well, well," said Boots, laughing. "I can certainly see how handy such a whistle might be! Thank you kindly, good mother, and if you ever get your nose caught again, you know who to call!"

Boots arrived at the King's palace and announced his intentions.

"I have come to win the Princess if she'll have me," he said. "And perhaps herd a few rabbits on the side." The guardsman brought Boots straight to the King; this day, the Princess sat beside him.

"Oh, yes indeed!" the King grinned. "Yes, I still need someone to herd my rabbits. But if you fail to keep the herd together, if you lose just one baby rabbit, you will get such a beating as will turn you black and blue."

"Righty-o, King," said Boots. "But let us not forget the rest of the bargain. If I keep the rabbits safely together, I win the Princess to wife, if she'll have me. Otherwise it is not worth the risk." Boots looked at the Princess. The Princess looked at Boots. She liked what she saw.

"Be off with you then!" said the King.

So Boots was taken out to the rabbit paddock, and there they were, all those bunnies hop hop hopping about. All morning Boots herded rabbits and in the afternoon he took them out to the hills. Once in the hills the rabbits kicked up their heels and away they ran.

"So that's the game, is it?" said Boots. "Well, I am willing to play it, too."

He took out his whistle and blew a tune on the right end of it, and away those bunnies flew, as though a strong wind had blown them. Then Boots threw himself under a tree and fell asleep in the shade. When he awoke it was time to bring the rabbits back to the castle, but not one of them was in sight.

Boots sat up, shook the hair out of his eyes, and blew on the wrong end of the pipe. Immediately there was the whole herd of rabbits before him, drawn up in ranks just like soldiers. Not even one of the smallest bunnies was missing.

"Very good!" said Boots. "And now we'll be going home again."

Off he set for the palace, driving the rabbits before him, and as soon as he came near he could see the King standing on the steps, waiting for him with a stout cudgel in his hand.

When the King saw the whole herd come hopping home, turning into the paddock as tame as sheep, he could hardly believe his eyes. He hurried over and began to count them. He counted them over and over again, and not one was missing.

Well, Boots had brought them all back safely that time, but the question was whether he could do it again.

Boots thought he could. Indeed, he was sure he could. So the next morning off he went.

That day things happened just as they had before. When the King found the lad had brought the whole herd home again for the second time he was greatly troubled, for he had no mind to give the Princess to Boots for a bride. So the third day he bade the Princess go out to the hills and hide herself among the bushes and see how it was that Boots managed to keep the rabbits together. The Princess promised to do her best.

So she did. She hid back of the bushes; she saw Boots come tramping up the hill with the bunnies frisking before him; she saw him blow them away with his pipe as though they were so many dry leaves in the wind, and then, after he had had a nap, she saw him blow them together again.

A promise is a promise, so the Princess must and would have that pipe. She came out from the bushes and offered to buy it. She offered ten dollars for it.

"No, Princess. Some cool water to drink?"

"Fifty?" asked the Princess as she sipped.

"No, Princess," said Boots. "Here, sit on my jacket and rest in the shade."

"A hundred?" asked the Princess, looking at the bright blue sky through the bright green leaves.

"No, Princess," said Boots, "but I tell you what I will do. I will sell you the pipe for a hundred dollars if you will give me one sweet kiss for every dollar paid."

The Princess looked at Boots. She liked what she saw. She paid Boots a hundred bright silver dollars, and she gave him a hundred sweet kisses right there on the hillside, with no one to see but the rabbits.

Then, because a promise is a promise, she took the pipe and ran home with it, but small good it did her. Just as she reached the palace steps the pipe slipped out of her fingers as though it had been buttered, and look as she might she could not find it again.

That was because Boots had wished it back to himself. At that very moment he was on his way home with the pipe in his pocket and the rabbits hopping before him in lines like soldiers.

The Princess told her father her story, leaving out the kisses. The King went to see the Queen.

"The Princess is young and foolish," said he. "She must have lost the pipe on the hillside, and no doubt that blasted Boots has it back by this time. Go buy it from him, and once you have your fingers on it, don't lose it!"

So the Queen went out to the hillside with two hundred dollars in her pocket and hid herself in the bushes. She saw Boots blow the bunnies away and lie down to sleep and afterward blow them together again in a twinkling.

Then she came out from the bushes. Boots leapt to his feet when he saw her.

"Your Majesty!" He bowed.

"Boots, I must have that pipe," the Queen said sternly.

"Your Majesty, I would cross mountains for you, sail stormy seas, lay my cape if I had one over a puddle, but I cannot sell you my pipe."

"A hundred dollars."

"No, regretfully, Your Majesty," answered Boots.

"One hundred and fifty."

"No, regretfully, really, Your Majesty."

"Two hundred dollars."

"No, regretfully, really, Your Majesty, but, oh, you would never . . ."

"What?" said the Queen.

"Well, my mother died when I was a baby, and I have never known a mother's kiss."

Poor boy, thought the Queen, and in the end Boots sold the pipe to the Queen for two hundred dollars and fifty motherly kisses on the forehead, and the Queen hoped the King would never hear of it. She took the pipe and ran home, thinking all the while what a nice boy that Boots was, really, so polite. And no mother, poor lamb. Nothing wrong with him that a decent haircut wouldn't fix, really.

The Queen fared no better than the Princess, however, for just before she reached the palace the pipe disappeared from her fingers, and what became of it she did not know.

When the King heard that, he was a wroth and angry man. If he once had the pipe in his hands there would be no losing it again, of that he felt very sure. So he mounted his old mare Whitey and rode over to the hillside. There he hid himself among the bushes, and he hid old Whitey there with him, and he watched until he had seen all he had been told. Then he came out and tried to strike a bargain with the lad.

But Boots would not sell the pipe. The King offered him three hundred dollars, and four hundred dollars, and five hundred dollars for it, and still Boots said no.

"Listen!" said Boots suddenly. "If you'll go over there in the bushes and kiss old Whitey on the mouth five-and-twenty times, I'll sell you the pipe for five hundred dollars, but not otherwise."

That was a thing the King was loath to do, for it ill befitted a king to kiss a horse, but have the pipe he must; and besides there was nobody there to see him do it but Boots, and he did not count.

So the King kissed old Whitey five-and-twenty times and gave Boots five hundred silver dollars. Boots gave him the pipe, and the

King mounted and rode away with it, well pleased with his own cleverness. He held the pipe tight in one hand and the bridle in the other. "No danger of my losing it as the Queen and the Princess did," thought he. Scarcely had the King reached the palace steps when the pipe slipped through his fingers like water, and what became of it he did not know.

When Boots drove the rabbits home that evening he had the pipe safely in his pocket, though nobody knew it.

And now how about the Princess? Would the King keep his promise and give her to a rabbit herder for a wife? But that was a thing the King could not bear to think of.

So in the end this is what the King said. The Princess was a very clever girl, and she must have a clever lad for a husband. If Boots could tell bigger stories than the Princess, then he should have her for a wife, but if she could tell bigger stories than he, then he should have three red strips cut from his back and be beaten all the way home.

Boots looked at the Princess. The Princess looked at Boots. She liked what she saw.

"The Princess is well worth such a wild risk," said Boots. "I agree."

Then the Princess smiled and began. "I looked out of my window," said she, "and there was a tree that grew straight up to the sky, and the fruit of it was diamonds and pearls and rubies. I reached out and picked them and made myself such a necklace as never was, and I might have it yet only I leaned over the well to look at myself in the waters, and the necklace fell off, and there it lies still at the bottom of the well for anyone who cares to dive for it."

"That is a pretty story!" said Boots, "but I can tell a better. When I was herding rabbits the Princess came up on the hill and gave me a hundred bright silver dollars and a hundred kisses as well, one for every dollar."

Then the King scowled till his brows met, and the Princess looked at Boots with a sparkling eye.

"Oh, a pretty story indeed!" laughed she, but then it was her turn again.

"I went to see my godmother, and she took me for a ride in a golden coach drawn by six fleas, and the fleas were as big as horses, and they went so fast we were back again a day before we started."

"That's a very good story," said Boots, "but here's a better. The Queen came out on the hillside and made me a present of two hundred dollars, and she kissed me."

The Princess frowned.

"Fifty motherly kisses," Boots hastened to add, "out of pity for a poor motherless lad."

"Is that true?" said the King to the Queen, and his face was red as a radish.

"It's a very good story," comforted the Queen, "and you must allow that it is."

Then the Princess tried again.

"I had six suitors, and I cared for one no more than another, but the seventh one was a demon, and he would have had me whether or no. He would have flown away with me before this, but I caught his tail in the crack of the door, and he howled most horribly. There he is still, if you care to look, unless he has vanished in a puff of smoke."

"Now it is my turn," said Boots, "and you may believe this or not, but it's mostly true. The King came up on the hillside and kissed the old white mare twenty-five times. I was there and I saw. He kissed her twenty-five times, and he gave me five hundred silver dollars not to tell."

"There's not a word of truth in it. It's the biggest story I ever heard," blustered the King.

"Very well, then I have won," said Boots. The Princess clapped her hands.

"We marry in one week," the Princess declared.

And married they were, for the Princess would not be denied.

The Queen arranged a great feast for the wedding, with plenty of cake and ale flowing like water. I was there, and I ate and drank with the best of them.

Pfst! There goes a mouse. Catch it and you may make a fine big cloak of its skin—and that's a story, too.

The Wild Geese

Ages 12–14. Retold by Janice M. Del Negro from *Grimm's Fairy Stories*, illustrated by John B. Gruelle and R. Emmett Owen (Cupples and Leon, 1922).

This tale can be found in a number of sources, including Hans Christian Andersen and traditional ballads. Sometimes the brothers are turned into ravens, sometimes into swans, and sometimes into wild ducks. This is a romantic tale with many traditional archetypes that may be familiar to listeners. Remember that ritual openings such as "Once upon a time" are a signal to your listeners that the story is about to begin. Don't throw the phrase away; take a breath and take your time.

Once upon a time a King hunting in a deep forest pursued his prey so hotly that none of his companions could follow him. Night fell, and the King, suddenly noticing the darkness, realized he was lost. Turning to search out a path, he was startled to see an old woman.

"What are you doing here, old woman? The night falls dark and cold."

"Oh, my poor lost King," the woman said. "Without me you will never find your way out of the wood. Do not fear. I will help you . . . if you will make my daughter your Queen. Come, she waits for you."

The old woman led the King to her cottage, where her daughter was sitting by the fire. The king saw at once that she was very beautiful, but there was something not quite right, for he could not look at her without a cold shudder. But she was very beautiful, and he did need to get out of the wood, so he took the maiden upon his horse, the old woman showed him the path, and the

King arrived safely at his palace, where the wedding was shortly celebrated.

Now this King had been married once before, and had children by his first wife, seven boys and one girl, whom he loved above everything else in the world. Sadly, the children's mother was dead, and the king's new wife, well, she was not quite right. She was so not right that the King was afraid that she might do his children harm. He hid them in a lonely castle in the midst of the deep forest. The King himself could not have found this castle but for a gift from a wise woman: a magical ball of cotton which, when the King threw it before him, unrolled and showed him the way.

The King went so often to see his dear children that his new Queen became suspicious. She followed him, and discovered the secret of the King's sons, and of the ball of cotton that showed him the way. The Queen made some fine silk shirts, and one day, when the King was gone hunting, she took the shirts and went to the castle in the forest. She needed no ball of cotton to show her the way, for she was her mother's daughter. The King's sons, seeing someone coming in the distance, thought it was their father and ran to meet him. The Queen threw over each boy a silk shirt. When the shirts touched their bodies, the boys were changed into wild geese, which flew off in a rush of wings. The Queen went home, thinking she was free of her stepchildren and now the King would love her alone. But the King's daughter had not run to greet the Queen, and the Queen did not see her.

The following day the King went to visit his children, but he found only his daughter, Valeria.

"Where are your brothers?" asked the King.

"Ah, dear father," Valeria replied, "a dark woman came out of the forest and changed them into wild geese, and they flew off over the forest. See? Here are the feathers they dropped as they flew away."

The King grieved for his sons, and, in fear for his daughter, he took her home with him. Upon reaching his own castle the King called his wife, and bade her to care for Valeria as if she were the Queen's own. The Queen's fury was hidden from the King, but not from Valeria.

"There is something not quite right about this Queen," thought Valeria. "I must go and seek my brothers."

When night came Valeria slipped from the castle walls and escaped into the deep woods. When his daughter was found missing, the King thought the worst, and the Queen discovered just how fierce the rage of a grieving father could be.

Valeria was as safe as anyone wandering the woods alone can be. She walked all night long, and most of the next day, until she was so weary she could walk no further. She saw a rough-looking hut, and going in, she found a room with seven beds. She crawled underneath a bed and prepared to sleep on the hard earth. Just as the sun was setting, she heard a rustling, and seven wild geese flew in the window. They settled on the ground and one by one their goose feathers slipped from them like silk shirts. Valeria knew them at once for her brothers, and gladly crept out from under the bed. Her brothers were not less glad to see her, but their joy was short.

"You cannot stay here," said they to her. "This is a robbers' hiding place and if they find you they will murder you."

"Can you not protect me, then?" inquired Valeria.

"No," they replied, "for we can only lay aside our feathers at twilight and for that time alone we regain our human form. When darkness falls we are geese once more."

"There must be some way to free you from this wicked spell!" Valeria cried.

"Dear sister, there is a way, but it is impossible," said her eldest brother. "No one can do it."

"Tell me just the same," Valeria demanded.

"Seven shirts made from the thorns of starflowers will restore our humanity, but she who makes them must make no sound while sewing them, must weep no tears, no matter how long it takes. Should there fall a single word from her lips, a single tear from her eyes, then all her labor will be in vain." Just as the brother finished speaking, twilight passed, and in a flash of feathers and down, the geese flew out of the cottage, their wings beating the air.

When Valeria's brothers were gone, she left the cottage and went deeper into the forest. There she passed the night in a hollow deep in the wide branches of an ancient tree. The next morning she gathered the starflowers needed to make the shirts that would free her brothers. She retreated to her nest in the tree, and there she sat, intent upon nothing but her work. The next twilight her brothers discovered her. The brothers brought Valeria water and nuts, berries and stolen bread, and in this way time passed as Valeria silently labored, shirt by shirt.

After she had passed some time there, it happened that the King of that country was hunting in the forest, and his huntsmen came beneath the tree in which Valeria sat. They called to her and asked, "Who are you, and what are you doing up in that tree?" She did not answer. "Come down," they said, "we will not harm you."

Valeria shook her head, and when they kept asking her questions, she threw down her gold necklace, hoping they would take it and leave. They did not, so she threw down her jeweled belt, and finally her silver bracelets, but their curiosity was too great. At last the lead huntsman himself climbed the tree and carried Valeria down and took her before the King.

The King asked her, "Who are you? What were you doing up in that tree?"

But Valeria, thinking only of her brothers, did not answer. He questioned her in all the languages that he knew, but she remained dumb as a fish. Still, the King's heart was touched, and he conceived for her a strong affection. He wrapped her in his cloak, and, placing her before him on his horse, took her to his castle. There he ordered rich garments to be made for her, and, although her beauty shone as sunbeams, not a word escaped her. The King placed her by his side at table, and there her dignified manners so won him that he said, "This Maiden will I marry, and no other in the world," and after some days he did just that. What Valeria thought of this no one knew, for not a word did she speak. She gathered starflowers in the royal gardens and worked on the shirts that would free her brothers.

Now, the King's mother was discontented with this marriage since it meant she was no longer a power in the court, and the King's mother spoke evil of the young Queen.

"Who knows whence this silent woman comes?" said the woman. "She who cannot speak is not worthy of a king." The King, however, would tolerate no criticism of his beloved wife.

A year after the wedding, when Queen Valeria brought her firstborn son into the world, the King's mother kidnapped him. Then she went to the King.

"Your wife, this silent sorceress, has murdered your firstborn son for some demonic rite! She is worthy of nothing but death!"

There was no proof, and the King would not believe it. He suffered no one to do any injury to his wife. The grief-stricken Valeria did not weep for her child but sat sewing at her shirts, ignoring everything else.

When a second child was born, the false old woman used the same deceit.

"Your second child, gone in the night! Who else but this silent mother has such a will for death? Any worthy woman would cry anguish at such a loss!"

But the King so loved his wife, he would not listen.

"Could my wife but speak and defend herself, her innocence would come to light." He suffered no one to do any injury to his wife. Valeria did not weep for her child but sewed shirts for her brothers, ignoring everything else.

But when the King's mother stole away the third child, again accusing the Queen, the King was obliged to give his wife up to be tried. Unable to speak in her own defense, the young Queen was condemned to suffer death by fire.

Because she was Queen, Valeria was prisoner in her rooms, not the royal dungeons. She did not eat or sleep, but worked on completing the seven shirts. When the time came for the sentence to be carried out, the seven shirts were ready, all but the last, which still needed the left sleeve. As Valeria was led to the scaffold, she draped the shirts over her arm. Just as the executioner raised the torch to light the fire, seven wild geese came flying through the air and settled, wing to wing, upon the pile of wood that was to be the Queen's pyre.

The geese surrounded Valeria, and over each one she threw a starflower shirt. "My brothers!" she cried, and Valeria's brothers stood up in a surge of feathers, restored to their humanity. They were alive and well but for the youngest, who wore the seventh shirt and had a graceful wing instead of a left arm. Brothers and sister embraced, and Valeria turned to her King.

"Now I may speak, my dear husband. I am innocent! Your mother in her passion for power stole away our children and accused me of their murder."

The King's mother was without defense, for a faithful servant of the King, who had taken the children at the heartless woman's order, brought them forward now and proved Valeria true. The King's anger was terrible to behold. His wicked mother met the fate she had planned for Valeria, and the faithful servant was richly rewarded. The King and Queen were reunited with their children and the Queen was reunited with her brothers. Messages were sent to Valeria's father, and he hastened to a reunion that healed his heart. There was a royal feast for the entire castle, and they ate and they drank and were merry and of good cheer, on that day, the next day, and all the days that came after.

BEYOND THE LEGACY

Storytelling Now

A graduate library school student came to storytelling class one night describing a regional library conference she had attended, in which the featured speaker told his audience, "Storytelling is dead." Librarians in school and public libraries no longer told stories to any audience but preschoolers, and those stories were not told, but read aloud. This comment was a great surprise to the storytelling students I taught then and continue to teach now. The comment surprised the librarians on the PUBYAC electronic discussion list as well, who, from North Carolina to California, Illinois to New York, chimed in with their descriptions of oral storytelling to everyone from grade school students to adults.

Storytelling is still taught in graduate schools of library and information science, is still an event at the American Library Association's Annual Conference, and is still actively practiced in libraries, classrooms, museums, bars, and coffeehouses across the United States and around the world. In the frenetic isolation and illusory community so often created by too many technological connections, storytelling creates a still and quiet place, a commonality of experience, a community of listeners. There is little that can match the elegant clarity of effective oral storytelling, the transfer of story from teller to listener without props, technology, or text.

The library tradition of storytelling grew from the professional desire to connect listening children to story as a way to open the doors to literature, narrative, and language. Effie Power, influential author of *Library Service for Children* (1930), said that the primary purpose for storytelling in the school or public library setting is to interpret literature for children and to inspire them to read it for themselves. Storytelling is a valuable method for giving children a love of language and an awareness of the spoken word.

Despite fierce competition for the attention of youngsters, storytelling remains an undeniable presence in school and public libraries, in classrooms, and at community events. Librarian storytellers are forceful advocates for traditional and other literature, telling stories that motivate listeners to search out the books from which those stories come. A strong, culturally inclusive folktale collection is a place where many voices can be heard, literally as well as figuratively. Storytelling in school and public libraries serves not only as a bridge for accessing the library collection but as a bridge for accessing the global community.

All types of traditional literature are valuable as an aesthetic experience, but when told aloud, they also become valuable in ways that appeal to more pragmatic minds. The connections between storytelling and pre-literacy and literacy skills have long been noted. Educational benefits of storytelling for listeners include increased phonological awareness, familiarity with narrative patterns, enhanced listening skills, enhanced memory, and a better understanding of the sequencing of events. Folktales, because of their narrative structure, repetitive language elements, and predictability, are ideal tools for literacy and language development.

Research continues to support oral storytelling as a tool for literacy in terms of vocabulary acquisition, listening skills, comprehension, and the ability to impose narrative order upon both text and life experiences (see Chasse, *Telling Tales*, and Haven, *Story Proof: The Science behind the Startling Power of Story*). Reading motivation is the holy grail of youth services librarianship, and storytelling is a proven technique for connecting children, stories, and books. Storytelling is a community builder: a group with nothing in common listens to the same story and suddenly they have a shared experience. Anecdotal evidence on the efficacy of storytelling is not hard to find. Ruth Sawyer, a powerfully influential storyteller, tells about an encounter she had with a child and a story in *The Way of the Storyteller* (1977). When 16-year-old Sawyer visited Boston with her parents, she babysat for the 7-year-old daughter of their hosts. During the daytime all was well, but when night fell the child became frightened and uneasy. At bedtime, she would not go to bed until Sawyer promised to stay with her and keep a light burning. Sawyer offered a story, but the child resisted; she hated stories as much as she hated the dark, especially stories with witches, giants, and ogres in them. "How about fairies?" Sawyer asked. "They're elegant." Sawyer then told the story of the boy who gathered herbs by moonlight so his mother would be healed. "It will sound better if I put out the light." She told the story three times. The next night it was the same, and the next, until "dark came gently, with it the stars, the call of the screech owl, and all the little sounds of earth that came with spring. Together we felt the comfortable darkness fold us in." Years later Sawyer met her charge in a cafeteria. The girl, now an eighth-grader, cried out, "I know who you are! You're the girl who made me like the dark" (Sawyer, 1977, pp. 83–84).

In a world where tangibles and intangibles are increasingly at odds, where information is both ephemeral and powerful, story has a crucial place. In libraries and classrooms, storytelling becomes a way to forge connections among listeners. Storytelling creates a shared common experience, promotes empathy, and provides a means of making sense of the world.

The library storytelling tradition features many prominent professional women and men who, in the twentieth century, saw in storytelling a way to inspire the children in their charge to read folktales, a term that can refer to many forms of traditional literature, including myths (narratives about a person, place, or event) and legends (narratives about gods or culture heroes; see Greene and Del Negro, *Storytelling: Art and Technique*, pp. 441–442). There are numerous librarian storytellers, such as Carol Birch, Ellin Greene, Betsy Hearne, Margaret Read MacDonald, and Judy Sierra, who shared and continue to share their expertise in books, articles, and stories. Their work—and their dedication to storytelling—serves as a guide to the many facets of storytelling in the library and school setting.

Librarian storytellers, such as Augusta Baker, Mary Gould Davis, Virginia Haviland, and others, not only told stories but also retold and compiled folktales for others to read and tell. There's a lengthy list of contemporary storytellers and folktale retellers who continue to enrich the store of folktales available to those of us telling stories in the classroom and in the library: Alma Flor Ada, Heather Forest, Shelley Fu, Ji-Li Jiang, Dan Keding, Julius Lester, Lise Lunge-Larsen, Hugh Lupton, Alice McGill, Patricia McKissack, Won-Ldy Paye, Tim Tingle, Donna Washington, Jane Yolen, and many others.

The popularity of the traditional folktale for youth has swung back and forth throughout the history of children's literature: folktales are too violent for young listeners and readers; folktales are unrealistic and give children a skewed vision of the world; female characters in folktales are passive and boring; folktales published for youth are not culturally authentic. The pendulum swings: folktales help children develop their imaginations and creativity; heroines and heroes in folktales teach listeners to persevere and overcome obstacles; the narrative schema of traditional folktales can teach children basic story structure and assist in the acquisition of literacy skills; folktales can help connect children to their own and other cultures. It is true that the storyteller in a library or classroom cannot duplicate the experience of hearing a traditional storyteller in an authentic cultural arena, just as it is true that telling one folktale does not provide an encompassing view of a culture. That being understood, telling well-sourced folktales from many cultures raises awareness of those cultures and promotes pride in the cultural heritage of individual listeners. The shared folktale provides listeners with a common experience and creates unity from the diversity of many.

Any form of literature that can be told with aesthetic authority is the source from which we draw as storytellers. When telling folktales, however, we must be aware that these tales have histories, varied sources, and, sometimes, a plethora of retellers, all of which go into making the story what it is today. Providing credit for the known author of a story, book, or poem is simple; we show the book, we tell the name, we connect the writer, the book, and the reader or listener.

With traditional tales we must be aware that folktales in collections and picture books, online and recorded, were not always collected with academic rigor, nor did collectors and retellers necessarily have the cachet of cultural insiders. The tales were taken from the oral and locked into print in the versions deemed most suitable at the time they were collected. The tales underwent change in the passing from voice to page to eye, and they undergo change yet again when we lift them from the page and give them once more to air and ear.

We can talk concretely about folktales—how they are structured, how they traveled, how folktale themes echo from culture to culture—but there is no definitive version of a folktale, no original version, no template. Printed folktales are evaluated through aesthetic, folkloric, and pragmatic viewpoints tempered by the sociopolitical environments in which the stories are collected and retold. Concerns about authenticity in folktales have been addressed by storyteller, librarian, and scholar Betsy Hearne, who has written extensively on the selection, evaluation, and use of the folktale.

When we return to the basics we are left with the story itself and with our retelling of it. How do we tell stories today? How do we take traditional tales from the past and make them relevant to new listeners? The story changes as it moves from the page to the air, from what we find—notes, origins, variants, cultural information—to what we tell and how we tell it. As storytellers today, we participate in centuries of retelling, adapting stories to suit the present need.

Stories are universal; every culture has them. Some cultures have more formal rules than others regarding the telling of stories. Just as there is no one book to guide you to storytelling, there is no one set of rules that applies to every story situation. The more you tell stories, the more storytellers you hear and work with, the deeper your understanding of contemporary storytelling issues and ethics will become. Join your local storytelling guild; go online and look for your regional organization; visit the website of the National Storytelling Network. Seek out the generous souls who encourage you to tell, who offer their experience to enrich yours.

Becoming a storyteller is a process. Storytellers, green and seasoned, must consider a spectrum of issues—from research to selection to retelling—and make their own decisions based on their experience, knowledge, and affinity with the story. If you start telling stories today, you will know a great deal more a year from now about how stories work. Storytelling is a subtle passion that takes over your life; you will begin to see pattern and story wherever you go.

In one sense the act of storytelling transcends the story itself. During a storytelling experience the storyteller and the listeners create the story together, synthesizing a dynamic multitude of variables that results in a distinct, one-time-only occurrence, a story that will not be told the same way ever again. The style of the individual teller combines with the response of the individual listener and the response of the listening group as a whole to make each tale, no matter how many times it is told, fresh and new.

I took a storytelling class in graduate library school. My professor told me that preschoolers needed the visual stimulation of the picture book in order to connect to story. I believed that wholeheartedly, only to discover that 3- to 6-year-olds connect to story just fine, whether through the visual experience of the picture book or the auditory experience of an oral tale.

My professor told me something else: never tell a story you don't like. I didn't believe that, but I should have, because in thirty years of telling stories, it is one of the truest things I have learned. Learning a story for a pedantic purpose is a waste of your time; you won't like it, your listeners won't like it, and you won't ever tell it again. Remember that with a little imagination any story can fit any theme, so tell stories that speak to you, make you laugh, make you think, make you sigh. Remember that the listening ear is very forgiving; a strong opening and satisfying conclusion will go a long way to ensuring contented listeners, no matter what happens between the beginning and the end. Remember that storytelling is a conversation, not a performance, intimate and specific.

Be brave. Be true. Tell stories.

Suggested Readings

Ada, Alma Flor. *Tales Our Abuelitas Told: A Hispanic Folktale Collection*. With F. Isabel Campoy. Atheneum, 2006.

Baker, Augusta. *The Golden Lynx and Other Tales*. Lippincott, 1960.

———. *The Talking Tree*. Illus. by Johannes Troyer. Lippincott, 1955.

Cai, Mingshui. *Multicultural Literature for Children and Young Adults: Reflections on Critical Issues*. Contributions to the Study of World Literature, no. 116. Greenwood, 2002.

Chasse, Emily S. *Telling Tales*. Neal-Schuman, 2009.

Davis, Mary Gould. *A Baker's Dozen: Thirteen Stories to Tell and to Read Aloud*. Harcourt Brace, 1930.

Forest, Heather. *Wonder Tales from Around the World*. August House, 1997.

Fu, Shelley. *Ho Yi the Archer and Other Classic Chinese Tales*. Illus. by Joseph F. Abboreno. Linnet Books, 2001.

Haase, Donald, ed. *Fairy Tales and Feminism: New Approaches*. Wayne State University Press, 2004.

Haven, Kendall. *Story Proof: The Science behind the Startling Power of Story*. Libraries Unlimited, 2007.

Haviland, Virginia. *Favorite Fairy Tales Told Around the World*. Little, Brown, 1985.

Hearne, Betsy. "The Bones of Story." *Horn Book Magazine* (January/February 2005): 39–47.

———. "Cite the Source: Reducing Cultural Chaos in Picture Books, Part One." *School Library Journal*, 7 (1993): 22–27.

———. "Respect the Source: Reducing Cultural Chaos in Picture Books, Part Two." *School Library Journal*, 8 (1993): 33–37.

———. "Swapping Tales and Stealing Stories: The Ethics and Aesthetics of Folklore in Children's Literature." *Library Trends*, 47, no. 3 (Winter 1999): 509–528.

Jiang, Ji-Li. *The Magical Monkey King: Classic Chinese Tales*. Illus. by Hui-Hui Su-Kennedy. HarperCollins, 2002.

Keding, Dan. *The United States of Storytelling: Folktales and True Tales from the Western States*. Libraries Unlimited, 2010.

Kuykendall, Leslee Farish, and Brian W. Sturn. "We Said Feminist Fairy Tales, Not Fractured Fairy Tales!" *Children and Libraries: The Journal of the Association for Library Services to Children*, 5, no. 3 (2007): 38.

Lester, Julius. *Tales of Uncle Remus: The Adventures of Brer Rabbit*. Illus. by Jerry Pinkney. Dial, 1987.

Lunge-Larsen, Lise. *The Troll with No Heart in His Body and Other Tales of Trolls from Norway*. Houghton Mifflin, 1999.

Lupton, Hugh. *Tales of Mystery and Magic*. Illus. by Agnese Baruzzi. Barefoot Books, 2010.

MacDonald, Margaret Read. *Earth Care: World Folktales to Talk About*. Linnet Books/ShoeString, 1999.

———. *Look Back and See: Twenty Lively Tales for Gentle Tellers*. H. W. Wilson, 1991.

McGill, Alice. *Sure as Sunrise: Stories of Bruh Rabbit and His Walkin' Talkin' Friends*. Houghton, 2004.

McKissack, Patricia. *Porch Lies: Tales of Slicksters, Tricksters and Other Wily Characters*. Schwartz and Wade, 2006.

Power, Effie. *Library Service for Children*. American Library Association, 1930.

Sawyer, Ruth. *The Way of the Storyteller*. Penguin, 1977.

Seale, Doris, and Beverly Slapin. *A Broken Flute: The Native Experience in Books for Children*. Oyate, 2005.

Sierra, Judy. *Can You Guess My Name? Traditional Tales Around the World*. Clarion, 2002.

———. *Nursery Tales Around the World*. Illus. by Stefano Vitale. Clarion, 1996.

Slapin, Beverly, and Doris Seale. *Through Indian Eyes: The Native Experience in Books for Children*. 3rd ed. New Society, 1992.

RESOURCES FOR RESEARCHING FOLKTALES AND STORYTELLING

Aarne, Antti. *The Types of the Folktale: A Classification and Bibliography*. Translated and revised by Stith Thompson. Academia Scientiarum Fennica, 1995.

Ashliman, D. L. *A Guide to Folktales in the English Language: Based on the Aarne-Thompson Classification System*. Greenwood, 1987.

Bendix, Regina, and Galit Hasan-Rokem. *A Companion to Folklore*. Wiley-Blackwell, 2012.

Briggs, Katherine M. *A Dictionary of British Folk-Tales in the English Language*. Indiana University Press, 1991.

———. *An Encyclopedia of Fairies*. Pantheon, 1978.

Brinkerhoff, Shirley. *Contemporary Folklore*. Mason Crest, 2003.

Brunvand, Jan Harold. *Encyclopedia of Urban Legends*. ABC-CLIO, 2001.

———. *The Vanishing Hitchhiker: American Urban Legends and Their Meanings*. Norton, 1981.

Dance, Daryl Cumber, ed. *From My People: 400 Years of African Folklore.* Norton, 2002.

Eastman, Mary. *Index to Fairy Tales, Myths and Legends.* Faxon, 2008. Supplements 1 and 2, 1937, 1952.

Greene, Ellin, and George Shannon. *Storytelling: A Selected Annotated Bibliography.* Garland, 1986.

Haase, Donald, ed. *The Greenwood Encyclopedia of Folktales and Fairy Tales.* Greenwood, 2008.

Ireland, Norma Olin, comp. *Index to Fairy Tales, 1949–1972, Including Folklore, Legends, and Myths in Collections, Third Supplement.* Scarecrow, 1973.

———. *Index to Fairy Tales, 1973–1977, Including Folklore, Legends, and Myths in Collections, Fourth Supplement.* Scarecrow, 1985.

Ireland, Norma Olin, and Joseph W. Sprug, comps. *Index to Fairy Tales, 1978–1986, Including Folklore, Legends, and Myths in Collections, Fifth Supplement.* Scarecrow, 1989.

Kallen, Stuart A. *Urban Legends.* Lucent Books, 2006.

Leach, Maria, ed. *Funk and Wagnall's Standard Dictionary of Folklore, Mythology and Legend.* Harper, 1984.

Leeming, David A., ed. *Storytelling Encyclopedia: Historical, Cultural, and Multiethnic Approaches to Oral Traditions Around the World.* Oryx, 1997.

MacDonald, Margaret Read. *The Storyteller's Sourcebook: A Subject, Title and Motif Index to Folklore Collections for Children.* Neal-Schuman, Gale Research, 1982.

———. *The Storyteller's Sourcebook: A Subject, Title and Motif Index to Folklore Collections for Children, 1983–1999.* Gale Cengage, 2001.

Prahlad, Anand. *The Greenwood Encyclopedia of African American Folklore.* Greenwood, 2005.

Reynolds, Dwight F. *Arab Folklore: A Handbook.* Greenwood, 2007.

Sherman, Josepha, ed. *Storytelling: An Encyclopedia of Mythology and Folklore.* M. E. Sharpe, 2008.

Sierra, Judy. *The Storyteller's Research Guide: Folktales, Myths, and Legends.* Folkprint, 1996.

Sprug, Joseph W. *Index to Fairy Tales, 1987–1992: Including 310 Collections of Fairy Tales, Folktales, Myths, and Legends, with Significant Pre-1987 Titles Not Previously Indexed.* Scarecrow, 1994.

Thompson, Stith. *The Folktale.* University of California Press, 1977.

———. *Motif-Index of Folk-Literature: Classification of Narrative Elements in Folktales, Ballads, Myths, Fables, Medieval Romances, Exempla, Fabliaux, Jest-books, and Local Legends.* Indiana University Press, 1956.

Ziegler, Elsie B. *Folklore: An Annotated Bibliography and Index to Single Editions.* Faxon, 1973.

STORYTELLING
HOW-AND-WHY BOOKS

Birch, Carol L. *The Whole Story Handbook: Using Imagery to Complete the Story Experience*. August House, 2000.

Bruchac, Joseph. *Tell Me a Tale: A Book about Storytelling*. Harcourt, 1997.

Bryant, Sara Cone. *How to Tell Stories to Children*. Houghton Mifflin, 1973. [Note: The 1915 edition is available as an e-book at http://etext .lib.virginia.edu/toc/modeng/public/BryTell.html.]

Cabral, Len. *Len Cabral's Storytelling Book*. Neal-Schuman, 1997.

Collins, Rives, and Pamela Cooper. *The Power of Story: Teaching through Storytelling*. 2nd ed. Gorsuch, 1997.

Dailey, Sheila. *Putting the World in a Nutshell: The Art of the Formula Tale*. H. W. Wilson, 1994.

Danoff, Susan. *The Golden Thread: Storytelling in Teaching and Learning*. Storytelling Arts, 2006.

de Las Casas, Dianne. *Tell Along Tales! Playing with Participation Stories*. Libraries Unlimited, 2011.

de Vos, Gail. *Storytelling for Young Adults: A Guide to Tales for Teens*. Libraries Unlimited, 2003.

———. *What Happens Next? Contemporary Urban Legends and Popular Culture*. Libraries Unlimited, 2012.

Ellis, Elizabeth. *From Plot to Narrative: A Step-by-Step Process of Story Creation and Enhancement*. Parkhurst Brothers, 2012.

Emerson, Laura S. *Storytelling, the Art and the Purpose*. Zondervan, 1959.

Freeman, Judy. *Once Upon a Time: Using Storytelling, Creative Drama, and Reader's Theater with Children in Grades PreK–6*. Libraries Unlimited, 2007.

Greene, Ellin. *Read Me a Story: Books and Techniques for Reading Aloud and Storytelling*. Preschool Publications, 1992.

———. *Storytelling: Art and Technique*. With Janice M. Del Negro. Libraries Unlimited, 2010.

Hamilton, Martha, and Mitch Weiss. *Children Tell Stories: Teaching and Using Storytelling in the Classroom*. Owen, 2005.

Haven, Kendall. *Story Proof: The Science behind the Startling Power of Story*. Libraries Unlimited, 2007.

Holt, David, ed. *The Storyteller's Guide*. With Bill Mooney. August House, 1996.

Lane, Marcia. *Picturing the Rose: A Way of Looking at Fairy Tales*. H. W. Wilson, 1994.

Livo, Norma J. *Bringing Out Their Best: Values Education and Character Development through Traditional Tales*. Libraries Unlimited, 2003.

———. *Who's Afraid . . . ? Facing Children's Fears with Folktales*. Libraries Unlimited, 1994.

MacDonald, Margaret Read. *Storyteller's Start-up Book: Finding, Learning, Performing and Using Folktales*. August House, 2006.

———. *Tell the World: Storytelling across Language Barriers*. Libraries Unlimited, 2008.

———. *Twenty Tellable Tales: Audience Participation Folktales for the Beginning Storyteller*. American Library Association, 2004.

McBride-Smith, Barbara. *Tell It Together: Foolproof Scripts for Story Theatre.* August House, 2001.

Norfolk, Bobby, and Sherry Norfolk. *The Moral of the Story: Folktales for Character Development.* August House, 1999.

Pellowski, Anne. *The World of Storytelling.* H. W. Wilson, 1990.

Roney, R. Craig. *The Story Performance Handbook.* Lawrence Erlbaum, 2001.

Sawyer, Ruth. *The Way of the Storyteller.* Viking, 1942.

Shedlock, Marie. *The Art of the Story-teller.* 3rd ed. Dover, 1951.

Sierra, Judy. *Twice Upon a Time.* H. W. Wilson, 1989.

Sima, Judy, and Kevin Cordi. *Raising Voices: Creating Youth Storytelling Groups and Troupes.* Libraries Unlimited, 2003.

Simms, Laura. *Our Secret Territory: The Essence of Storytelling.* Sentient, 2011.

Spaulding, Amy E. *The Wisdom of Storytelling in an Information Age: A Collection of Talks.* Scarecrow, 2004.

Stenson, Jane, ed. *The Storytelling Classroom: Applications across the Curriculum.* Libraries Unlimited, 2006.

———. *The Storytelling Classroom: Literacy Development in the Storytelling Classroom.* 2nd ed. Libraries Unlimited, 2009.

Stenson, Jane, and Sherry Norfolk. *Social Studies in the Storytelling Classroom: Exploring Our Cultural Voices and Perspectives.* Parkhurst Brothers, 2012.

Trostle-Brand, Susan, and Jeanne Donata. *Storytelling in Emergent Literacy: Fostering Multiple Intelligences.* Delmar, 2001.

Weir, Beth. *Introducing Children to Folktales.* Christopher-Gordon, 2001.

Wright, Jonatha. *Team Up! Tell in Tandem! A "How-To" Guide from Experienced Tandem Storytellers.* With Charlotte Blake Alston, Judith Black, et al. Presto, 2010.

Yolen, Jane. *Touch Magic: Fantasy, Faerie and Folklore in the Literature of Childhood.* Philomel, 1981.

Zipes, Jack. *The Oxford Companion to Fairy Tales*. Oxford University Press, 2000.

———. *Speaking Out: Storytelling and Creative Drama for Children*. Routledge, 2004.

FOLKTALE PICTURE BOOKS

These are single-tale volumes of folktales. Authors noted are retellers, adapters, or collectors; see available source notes in each volume for more specific cites or other notes.

Aardema, Verna. *Borreguita and the Coyote: A Tale from Ayutla, Mexico.* Illus. by Petra Mathers. Knopf, 1991.

———. *Koi and the Kola Nuts: A Tale from Liberia.* Illus. by Joe Cepeda. Atheneum, 1999.

———. *Traveling to Tondo: A Tale of the Nkundo of Zaire.* Illus. by Will Hillenbrand. Knopf, 1991.

———. *Who's in Rabbit's House?* Illus. by Leo and Diane Dillon. Dial, 1979.

———. *Why Mosquitoes Buzz in People's Ears.* Illus. by Leo and Diane Dillon. Puffin, 1978.

Andreasen, Dan. *The Giant of Seville.* Illus. by author. Abrams, 2007.

Artell, Mike. *Petite Rouge: A Cajun Red Riding Hood*. Illus. by Jim Harris. Penguin Putnam, 2001.

Asbjørnsen, Peter Christen, and Jørgen Moe. *East o' the Sun and West o' the Moon*. Retold by Naomi Lewis. Illus. by P. J. Lynch. Candlewick, 1992.

Aylesworth, Jim. *The Mitten*. Illus. by Barbara McClintock. Scholastic, 2009.

———. *The Tale of Tricky Fox: A New England Trickster Tale*. Illus. by Barbara McClintock. Scholastic, 2001.

Bang, Molly Garrett. *Wiley and the Hairy Man*. Illus. by author. Macmillan, 1976.

Bateman, Teresa. *Damon, Pythias, and the Test of Friendship*. Illus. by Layne Johnson. Albert Whitman, 2009.

Batt, Tanya Robyn. *The Faerie's Gift*. Illus. by Nicoletta Ceccoli. Barefoot Books, 2003.

Battle-Lavert, Gwendolyn. *The Shaking Bag*. Illus. by Aminah Brenda Lynn Robinson. Whitman, 2000.

Belpré, Pura. *Perez and Martina: A Puerto Rican Folktale*. Illus. by Carlos Sanchez. Viking, 1991.

Birdseye, Tom. *Soap! Soap! Don't Forget the Soap!* Illus. by Andrew Glass. Holiday House, 1993.

Brown, Marcia. *Once a Mouse*. Illus. by author. Simon and Schuster, 1972.

Bruchac, Joseph, and Gayle Ross. *The Story of the Milky Way: A Cherokee Tale*. Illus. by Virginia A. Stroud. Dial, 1995.

Bruchac, Joseph, and James Bruchac. *How Chipmunk Got His Stripes*. Illus. by Jose Aruego and Ariane Dewey. Dial, 2001.

———. *Rabbit's Snow Dance: A Traditional Iroquois Story*. Illus. by Jeff Newman. Dial, 2012.

———. *Raccoon's Last Race: A Traditional Abenaki Story*. Illus. by Jose Aruego and Ariane Dewey. Dial, 2004.

———. *Turtle's Race with Beaver: A Traditional Seneca Story*. Illus. by Jose Aruego and Ariane Dewey. Dial, 2003.

Bryan, Ashley. *The Cat's Purr*. Illus. by author. Simon and Schuster, 1985.

———. *The Dancing Granny*. Illus. by author. Simon and Schuster, 1987.

———. *Turtle Knows Your Name*. Illus. by author. Simon and Schuster, 1989.

Bynum, Eboni, and Roland Jackson. *Jamari's Drum*. Glazed tiles by Baba Wagué Diakité. Groundwood Books, 2004.

Casanova, Mary. *The Hunter: A Chinese Folktale*. Illus. by Ed Young. Atheneum, 2000.

Cleveland, Rob. *How Tiger Got His Stripes: A Folktale from Vietnam*. Illus. by Baird Hoffmire. August House, 2006.

Compton, Patricia A. *The Terrible EEK: A Japanese Tale*. Illus. by Sheila Hamanaka. Simon and Schuster, 1991.

Cooper, Susan. *The Selkie Girl*. Illus. by Warwick Hutton. Simon and Schuster, 1986.

———. *The Silver Cow: A Welsh Tale*. Illus. by Warwick Hutton. Simon and Schuster, 1983.

———. *Tam Lin*. Illus. by Warwick Hutton. Simon and Schuster, 1991.

Cullen, Lynn. *Little Scraggly Hair: A Dog on Noah's Ark*. Illus. by Jacqueline Rogers. Holiday House, 2003.

Day, Nancy Raines. *The Lion's Whiskers: An Ethiopian Folktale*. Illus. by Ann Grifalconi. Scholastic, 1995.

Dayrell, Elphinstone. *Why the Sun and Moon Live in the Sky*. Illus. by Blair Lent. Houghton Mifflin, 1990.

Deedy, Carmen Agra. *Martina, the Beautiful Cockroach: A Cuban Folktale*. Illus. by Michael Austin. Peachtree, 2007.

DeFelice, Cynthia. *Cold Feet*. Illus. by Robert Andrew Parker. DK, 2000.

———. *The Dancing Skeleton*. Illus. by Robert Andrew Parker. Macmillan, 1989.

———. *Nelly May Has Her Say*. Illus. by Henry Cole. Margaret Ferguson Books, 2013.

———. *One Potato, Two Potato*. Illus. by Andrea U'Ren. Farrar, Straus and Giroux, 2006.

Demi. *The Hungry Coat: A Tale from Turkey*. Illus. by author. McElderry, 2004.

Diakité, Baba Wagué. *The Hatseller and the Monkeys*. Illus. by author. Scholastic, 1999.

———. *The Hunterman and the Crocodile*. Illus. by author. Scholastic, 1997.

———. *The Magic Gourd*. Illus. by author. Scholastic, 2003.

———. *Mee-an and the Magic Serpent: A Story from Mali*. Illus. by author. Groundwood Books, 2006.

Divakaruni, Chitra. *Grandma and the Great Gourd: A Bengali Folktale*. Illus. by Susy Waters. Roaring Brook, 2013.

Doyle, Malachy. *Hungry! Hungry! Hungry!* Illus. by Paul Hess. Peachtree, 2000.

Duvall, Deborah. *How Rabbit Lost His Tail: A Traditional Cherokee Legend*. Illus. by Murv Jacob. University of New Mexico Press, 2003.

———. *Rabbit Goes Duck Hunting: A Traditional Cherokee Legend*. Illus. by Murv Jacob. University of New Mexico Press, 2004.

Echewa, Obinkaram. *The Magic Tree: A Folktale from Nigeria*. Illus. by E. B. Lewis. Morrow, 1999.

Ehlert, Lois. *Cuckoo/Cucú: A Mexican Folktale*. Illus. by author. Harcourt, 2000.

———. *Moon Rope: A Peruvian Folktale/Un lazo a la luna: Una leyenda peruana*. Illus. by author. Harcourt, 1992.

Eilenberg, Max. *Beauty and the Beast*. Illus. by Angela Barrett. Candlewick, 2006.

Emberley, Barbara. *The Story of Paul Bunyan*. Illus. by Ed Emberley. Simon and Schuster, 1994.

Fleming, Candace. *Clever Jack Takes the Cake*. Illus. by G. Brian Karas. Schwartz and Wade Books, 2010.

Forest, Heather. *Feathers: A Jewish Tale from Eastern Europe*. Illus. by Marcia Cutchin. August House, 2005.

Fowles, Shelley. *The Bachelor and the Bean*. Illus. by author. Farrar, Straus and Giroux, 2003.

Fox, Frank G. *Jean Lafitte and the Big Ol' Whale*. Illus. by Scott Cook. Farrar, Straus and Giroux, 2003.

Galdone, Paul. *The Town Mouse and the Country Mouse*. Illus. by author. Houghton Mifflin Harcourt, 2012.

Gershator, David, and Phillis Gershator. *Kallaloo! A Caribbean Tale*. Illus. by Diane Greenseid. Marshall Cavendish, 2005.

Gerson, Mary-Joan. *Why the Sky Is Far Away: A Nigerian Folktale*. Illus. by Carla Golembe. Little, Brown, 1992.

González, Lucía M. *The Bossy Gallito/El Gallo de Bodas*. Illus. by Lulu Delacre. Scholastic, 1994.

Gottschall, Jonathan. *The Storytelling Animal: How Stories Make Us Human*. Mariner Books, 2013.

Greene, Ellin. *The Little Golden Lamb*. Illus. by Rosanne Litzinger. Clarion, 2000.

Gregorowski, Christopher. *Fly, Eagle, Fly! An African Fable*. Illus. by Niki Daly. McElderry, 2000.

Griffin, Kitty, and Kathy Combs. *The Foot-Stomping Adventures of Clementine Sweet*. Illus. by Mike Wohnoutka. Clarion, 2004.

Grimm, Jacob, and Wilhelm Grimm. *Hansel and Gretel*. Illus. by Paul O. Zelinsky. Dutton, 1999.

———. *Ouch!* Retold by Natalie Babbitt. Illus. by Fred Marcellino. HarperCollins, 1998.

———. *Rapunzel*. Illus. by Paul O. Zelinsky. Dutton, 1997.

———. *Rumpelstiltskin*. Illus. by Paul O. Zelinsky. Dutton, 1986.

Hague, Michael. *Kate Culhane: A Ghost Story*. Illus. by author. SeaStar, 2001.

Hamilton, Martha, and Mitch Weiss. *The Well of Truth: A Folktale from Egypt*. Illus. by Tom Wrenn. August House, 2009.

Hamilton, Virginia. *Bruh Rabbit and the Tar Baby Girl*. Illus. by James Ransome. Blue Sky/Scholastic, 2003.

————. *Wee Winnie Witch's Skinny: An Original African American Scare Tale*. Illus. by Barry Moser. Scholastic, 2004.

Han, Suzanne Crowder. *The Rabbit's Escape*. Illus. by Yumi Heo. Henry Holt. 1995.

————. *The Rabbit's Judgment*. Illus. by Yumi Heo. Henry Holt, 1994.

Harper, Wilhelmina. *The Gunniwolf*. Illus. by Barbara Upton. Dutton, 2003.

Harrington, Janice. *Busy-Busy Little Chick*. Illus. by Brian Pinkney. Farrar, Straus and Giroux, 2013.

Hayes, Joe. *The Day It Snowed Tortillas/El día que nevaron tortillas*. Illus. by Antonio Castro L. Cinco Puntos Press, 2003.

————. *El Cucuy! A Bogeyman Cuento*. Illus. by Honorio Robledo. Cinco Puntos Press, 2001.

————. *Little Gold Star/Estrellita de Oro: A Cinderella Cuento*. Illus. by Gloria Osuna Perez and Lucia Angela Perez. Cinco Puntos Press, 2000.

————. *The Weeping Woman/La Llorona*. Illus. by Vicki Trego Hill and Mona Pennypacker. Cinco Puntos Press, 2004.

Hooks, William H. *Moss Gown*. Illus. by Donald Carrick. Houghton Mifflin, 1987.

Hort, Lenny *The Fool and the Fish*. Illus. by Gennady Spirin. Dial, 1990.

Huling, Jan. *Ol' Bloo's Boogie-Woogie Band and Blues Ensemble: A Bayou Version of "The Bremen Town Musicians."* Illus. by Henri Sørensen. Peachtree, 2010.

Hurst, Margaret M. *Grannie and the Jumbie: A Caribbean Tale*. Illus. by author. HarperCollins, 2001.

Hurston, Zora Neale. *The Six Fools*. Adapted by Joyce Carol Thomas. Illus. by Ann Tanksley. HarperCollins, 2006.

————. *The Three Witches*. Adapted by Joyce Carol Thomas. Illus. by Faith Ringgold. HarperCollins, 2006.

————. *What's the Hurry, Fox?* Adapted by Joyce Carol Thomas. Illus. by Bryan Collier. HarperCollins, 2004.

Husain, Shahrukh. *The Wise Fool*. Illus. by Micha Archer. Barefoot Books, 2011.

Isaacs, Anne. *Pancakes for Supper!* Illus. by Mark Teague. Scholastic, 2006.

Ishii, Momoko. *The Tongue-Cut Sparrow*. Illus. by Suekichi Akaba. Dutton, 1987.

Janisch, Heinz. *The Fire: An Ethiopian Folktale*. Illus. by Fabricio Vanden-Broeck. Groundwood Books, 2002.

Jiang, Ji-Li. *The Magical Monkey King*. Illus. by Hui-Hui Su-Kennedy. HarperCollins, 2002.

Johnson, Paul Brett. *Fearless Jack*. Illus. by author. McElderry, 2001.

———. *Jack Outwits the Giants*. Illus. by author. McElderry, 2002.

Johnson, R. Kikuko. *The Shark King: A Toon Book*. Illus.by author. TOON Books, 2012.

Kimmel, Eric A. *Anansi and the Moss-Covered Rock*. Illus. by Janet Stevens. Holiday House, 1990.

———. *Joha Makes a Wish: A Middle Eastern Tale*. Illus. by Omar Rayyan. Marshall Cavendish, 2010.

———. *Three Samurai Cats: A Story from Japan*. Illus. by Mordicai Gerstein. Holiday House, 2003.

Knutson, Barbara. *Love and Roast Chicken: A Trickster Tale from the Andes Mountains*. Illus. by author. Carolrhoda, 2004.

———. *Sungura and Leopard: A Swahili Trickster Tale*. Illus. by author. Little, Brown, 1993.

Krensky, Stephen. *Calamity Jane*. Illus. by Lisa Carlson. Millbrook, 2007.

———. *Pecos Bill*. Illus. by Paul Tong. Millbrook, 2007.

Kurtz, Jane. *Fire on the Mountain*. Illus. by E. B. Lewis. Simon and Schuster, 1994.

———. *In the Small, Small Night*. Illus. by Rachel Isadora. Greenwillow, 2005.

Kushner, Lawrence, and Gary Schmidt. *In God's Hands*. Illus. by Matthew J. Baek. Jewish Lights, 2005.

Laird, Elizabeth. *Beautiful Bananas*. Illus. by Liz Pichon. Peachtree, 2004.

Landman, Tanya. *Mary's Penny*. Illus. by Richard Holland. Candlewick, 2010.

Lang, Andrew. *Aladdin and the Wonderful Lamp*. Illus. by Errol Le Cain. Puffin, 1983.

Langton, Jane. *Salt: A Russian Folktale*. Illus. by Ilse Plume. Hyperion, 1992.

Lee, Jeanne M. *Toad Is the Uncle of Heaven: A Vietnamese Folktale*. Illus. by author. Henry Holt, 1989.

Levine, Arthur A. *The Boy Who Drew Cats: A Japanese Folktale*. Illus. by Frédéric Clément. Dial, 1994.

Lewis, J. Patrick. *The Frog Princess: A Russian Folktale*. Illus. by Gennady Spirin. Dial, 1994.

Lexau, Joan M. *Crocodile and Hen*. Illus. by Doug Cushman. Harper-Collins, 2001.

Lottridge, Celia Barber. *The Name of the Tree: A Bantu Folktale*. Illus. by Ian Wallace. Simon and Schuster, 1990.

Lunge-Larson, Lise. *The Race of the Birkebeiners*. Illus. by Mary Azarian. Houghton Mifflin, 2001.

MacDonald, Amy. *Please, Malese! A Trickster Tale from Haiti*. Illus. by Emily Lisker. Farrar, Straus and Giroux, 2002.

MacDonald, Margaret Read. *Conejito: A Folktale from Panama*. Illus. by Geraldo Valerio. August House, 2006.

———. *Fat Cat: A Danish Folktale*. Illus. by Julie Paschkis. August House, 2001.

———. *Go to Sleep, Gecko! A Balinese Folktale*. Illus. by Geraldo Valerio. August House, 2006.

———. *The Great Smelly, Slobbery, Small-Tooth Dog: A Folktale from Great Britain*. Illus. by Julie Paschkis. August House, 2007.

———. *Little Rooster's Diamond Button*. Illus. by Will Terry. Albert Whitman, 2007.

————. *Mabela the Clever*. Illus. by Tim Coffey. Albert Whitman, 2001.

————. *Surf War! A Folktale from the Marshall Islands*. Illus. by Geraldo Valerio. August House, 2009.

Maddern, Eric. *The King and the Seed*. Illus. by Paul Hess. Frances Lincoln Children's Books, 2009.

Maggi, María Elena. *The Great Canoe: A Kariña Legend*. Illus. by Gloria Calderón. Douglas and McIntyre, 2001.

Martin, Francesca. *Clever Tortoise: A Traditional African Tale*. Illus. by author. Candlewick, 2000.

Martin, Rafe. *The Language of Birds*. Illus. by Susan Gaber. Putnam, 2000.

McDermott, Gerald. *Monkey: A Trickster Tale from India*. Illus. by author. Houghton Mifflin Harcourt, 2011.

McGill, Alice. *Way Up and Over Everything*. Illus. by Jude Daly. Houghton, 2008.

Milligan, Bryce. *The Prince of Ireland and the Three Magic Stallions*. Illus. by Preston McDaniels. Holiday House, 2003.

Mollel, Tolowa M. *The Flying Tortoise: An Igbo Tale*. Illus. by Barbara Spurll. Houghton Mifflin, 1994.

Montileaux, Donald F. *Tatanka and the Lakota People: A Creation Story*. Illus. by author. South Dakota State Historical Press, 2006.

Nadimi, Suzan. *The Rich Man and the Parrot*. Illus. by Ande Cook. Albert Whitman, 2007.

Norfolk, Bobby, and Sherry Norfolk. *Anansi and the Sky Kingdom*. Illus. by Baird Hoffmire. August House, 2009.

Nunes, Susan. *Tiddalick the Frog*. Illus. by Ju-Hong Chen. Simon and Schuster, 1989.

Olaleye, Isaac O. *In the Rainfield: Who Is the Greatest?* Illus. by Ann Grifalconi. Blue Sky, 2000.

Olson, Arielle North. *Noah's Cats and the Devil's Fire*. Illus. by Barry Moser. Orchard, 1992.

O'Malley, Kevin. *The Great Race*. Illus. by author. Walker, 2011.

————. *Velcome.* Illus. by author. Walker, 1999.

Orgel, Doris. *Doctor All-Knowing: A Folk Tale from the Brothers Grimm.* Illus. by Alexandra Boiger. Atheneum, 2008.

Osborne, Mary Pope. *New York's Bravest.* Illus. by Steve Johnson and Lou Fancher. Knopf, 2002.

Padma, T. V. *The Cleverest Thief.* Illus. by Baird Hoffmire. August House, 2008.

Parnell, Fran. *Grint, Grunt, and Grizzle-Tail.* Illus. by Sophie Fatus. Barefoot Books, 2013.

Paye, Won-Ldy, and Margaret H. Lippert. *Head, Body, Legs: A Story from Liberia.* Illus. by Julie Paschkis. Henry Holt, 2002.

————. *Mrs. Chicken and the Hungry Crocodile.* Illus. by Julie Paschkis. Henry Holt, 2003.

————. *Talking Vegetables.* Illus. by Julie Paschkis. Henry Holt, 2006.

Philip, Neil. *Noah and the Devil: A Legend of Noah's Ark from Romania.* Illus. by Isabelle Brent. Clarion, 2001.

Pinkney, Jerry. *Puss in Boots.* Illus. by author. Dial Books for Young Readers, 2012.

Pirotta, Saviour. *Firebird.* Illus. by Catherine Hyde. Templar/Candlewick, 2010.

Poole, Josephine. *Snow White.* Illus. by Angela Barrett. Knopf, 1991.

Powell, Patricia Hruby. *Ch'ał Tó Yinílo': Frog Brings Rain.* Illus. by Kendrick Benally. Salina Bookshelf, 2006.

Quattlebaum, Mary. *Why Sparks Fly High at Dancing Point: A Colonial American Folktale.* Illus. by Leonid Gore. Farrar, Straus and Giroux, 2006.

Réascol, Sabina I. *The Impudent Rooster.* Illus. by Holly Berry. Dutton, 2004.

Root, Phyllis. *Aunt Nancy and the Bothersome Visitors.* Illus. by David Parkins. Walker, 2008.

Ross, Gayle. *How Turtle's Back Was Cracked: A Traditional Cherokee Tale.* Illus. by Murv Jacob. Dial, 1995.

————. *The Legend of the Windigo*. Illus. by Murv Jacob. Dial, 1996.

Rounds, Glen. *Three Little Pigs and the Big Bad Wolf*. Illus. by author. Holiday House, 1992.

Salley, Coleen. *Epossumondas Saves the Day*. Illus. by Janet Stevens. Harcourt, 2006.

San Souci, Robert D. *Little Pierre: A Cajun Story from Louisiana*. Illus. by David Catrow. Harcourt, 2003.

————. *Sukey and the Mermaid*. Illus. by Brian Pinkney. Simon and Schuster, 1992.

Sawyer, Ruth. *Journey Cake, Ho!* Illus. by Robert McCloskey. Puffin, 1978.

Schlitz, Laura Amy. *The Bearskinner: A Tale of the Brothers Grimm*. Illus. by Max Grafe. Candlewick, 2007.

Shannon, George. *Rabbit's Gift*. Illus. by Laura Dronzek. Harcourt, 2007.

Sharpe, Leah Marinsky. *The Goat-Faced Girl: A Classic Italian Folktale*. Illus. by Jane Marinsky. David R. Godine, 2009.

Shepard, Aaron. *The Monkey King: A Superhero Tale of China*. Skyhook, 2008.

————. *One-Eye! Two-Eyes! Three-Eyes! A Very Grimm Fairy Tale*. Illus. by Gary Clement. Simon and Schuster Children's Publishing, 2007.

Sierra, Judy. *The Beautiful Butterfly: A Folktale from Spain*. Illus. by Victoria Chess. Clarion, 2000.

————. *Tasty Baby Belly Buttons*. Illus. by Meilo So. Dragonfly, 2001.

So, Meilo. *Gobble, Gobble, Slip, Slop: A Tale of a Very Greedy Cat*. Illus. by author. Knopf, 2004.

Spirin, Gennady. *Goldilocks and the Three Bears*. Illus. by author. Marshall Cavendish, 2009.

Stampler, Ann Redisch. *The Wooden Sword: A Jewish Folktale from Afghanistan*. Illus. by Carol Liddiment. Albert Whitman, 2012.

Steptoe, John. *Mufaro's Beautiful Daughters: An African Tale*. Illus. by author. Morrow, 1993.

Stevens, Janet. *Tops and Bottoms*. Illus. by author. Harcourt, 1995.

Stewig, John. *Clever Gretchen*. Illus. by Patricia Wittmann. Marshall Cavendish, 2000.

———. *King Midas: A Golden Tale*. Illus. by Omar Rayyan. Holiday House, 1999.

———. *Mother Holly*. Illus. by Johanna Westerman. North-South, 2001.

———. *Whuppity Stoorie*. Illus. by Preston McDaniels. Holiday House, 2004.

Thompson, Pat. *Drat That Fat Cat!* Illus. by Ailie Busby. Levine/Scholastic, 2003.

Thomson, Sarah L. *Cinderella: Based on the Story by Charles Perrault*. Illus. by Nicoletta Ceccoli. Marshall Cavendish, 2012.

Uchida, Yoshiko. *The Wise Old Woman*. Illus. by Martin Springett. Simon and Schuster, 1994.

Washington, Donna. *A Big, Spooky House*. Illus. by Jacqueline Rogers. Jump at the Sun/Hyperion, 2000.

Wattenberg, Jane. *Henny-Penny*. Illus. by author. Scholastic, 2000.

Wheeler, Lisa. *Avalanche Annie: A Not-So-Tall Tale*. Illus. by Kurt Cyrus. Harcourt, 2003.

Willey, Margaret. *Clever Beatrice: An Upper Peninsula Conte*. Illus. by Heather M. Solomon. Atheneum, 2001.

———. *Clever Beatrice and the Best Little Pony*. Illus. by Heather M. Solomon. Atheneum, 2004.

Wolkstein, Diane. *Sun Mother Wakes the World: An Australian Creation Story*. Illus. by Bronwyn Bancroft. HarperCollins, 2004.

———. *White Wave: A Chinese Tale*. Illus. by Ed Young. Harcourt, 1996.

Wooldridge, Connie Nordheim. *The Legend of Strap Buckner: A Texas Tale*. Illus. by Andrew Glass. Holiday House, 2001.

Wright, Catherine. *Steamboat Annie and the Thousand-Pound Catfish*. Illus. by Howard Fine. Philomel Books, 2001.

Yep, Laurence. *The Man Who Tricked a Ghost*. Illus. by Isadore Seltzer. Bridgewater, 1993.

Yolen, Jane. *Tam Lin*. Illus. by Charles Mikolaycak. Harcourt, 1990.

Young, Ed. *Monkey King*. Illus. by author. HarperCollins, 2001.

Zitkala-Ša. *Dance in a Buffalo Skull*. Illus. by S. D. Nelson. Prairie Tales Series, no. 2. South Dakota State Historical Society Press, 2007.

Zunshine, Tatiana. *A Little Story about a Big Turnip*. Illus. by Evgeny Antonenkov. Pumpkin House, 2003.

FOLKTALE COLLECTIONS

These selected folktale collections serve as an introduction to the breadth of world folktales available in print. Some titles are specifically published for reading by youth, some are not; all titles listed here are resources for storytellers to find stories they might like to tell. Ideally you will look at several versions of the same tale and come up with your own version, one that suits your telling style, audience, and intent. The titles noted in the Resources for Researching Folktales and Storytelling section, particularly Margaret Read MacDonald's two editions of *The Storyteller's Sourcebook*, will help you locate tales, tale variants, and modern retellings. The authors noted here are retellers, adapters, collectors, or editors. Again, look for cites regarding specific story origins in each individual title.

Ada, Alma Flor. *Tales Our Abuelitas Told: A Hispanic Folktale Collection.* Atheneum, 2006.

Aesop. *Fox Tails: Four Fables from Aesop.* Retold by Amy Lowry. Holiday House, 2012.

Afanasyev, Alexander. *Russian Fairy Tales*. Illus. by Ivan Bilibin. Planet, 2012.

———. *Russian Fairy Tales*. Pantheon, 1976.

Aldana, Patricia. *Jade and Iron: Latin American Tales from Two Cultures*. Douglas and McIntyre, 1996.

Alley, Zoë. *There's a Princess in the Palace*. Roaring Brook, 2010.

———. *There's a Wolf at the Door*. Roaring Brook, 2008.

Almeida, Livia Maria de. *Brazilian Folktales*. Edited by Margaret Read MacDonald. Libraries Unlimited, 2006.

Arkhurst, Joyce. *The First Adventures of Spider: West African Folktales*. Illus. by Jerry Pinkney. Little, Brown, 2012.

Asbjørnsen, Peter Christen, and Jørgen Moe. *Norwegian Folktales*. Pantheon, 1982.

Asher, Linda, and Jean-Pierre Vernant. *The Universe, the Gods, and Men: Ancient Greek Myths*. HarperCollins, 2001.

Asimov, Isaac. *Legends, Folklore, and Outer Space*. Gareth Stevens, 2005.

Badoe, Adwoa. *The Pot of Wisdom: Ananse Stories*. Illus. by Baba Wagué Diakité. Douglas and McIntyre, 2001.

Baker, Augusta. *The Golden Lynx*. Lippincott, 1960.

———. *The Talking Tree*. Illus. by Johannes Troyer. Lippincott, 1955.

Baltuck, Naomi. *Apples from Heaven: Multicultural Folk Tales about Stories and Storytellers*. Linnet Books, 1995.

Barefoot, Daniel W. *Haunted Halls of Ivy: Ghosts of Southern Colleges and Universities*. John F. Blair, 2004.

Barton, Bob. *The Bear Says North: Tales from Northern Lands*. Illus. by Jirina Marton. Groundwood Books, 2003.

Bedard, Michael. *The Painted Wall and Other Strange Tales*. Tundra Books, 2003.

Bernier-Grand, Carmen T. *Shake It, Morena! And Other Folklore from Puerto Rico*. Millbrook, 2002.

Bierhorst, John. *The Dancing Fox: Arctic Folktales*. Morrow, 1997.

———. *Latin American Folktales: Stories from Hispanic and Indian Traditions*. Pantheon Books, 2002.

———. *The Whistling Skeleton: American Indian Tales of the Supernatural*. Collected by George Bird Grinnell. Four Winds, 1982.

Bruchac, Joseph. *The Boy Who Lived with the Bears and Other Iroquois Stories*. HarperCollins, 1995.

Bruchac, Joseph, and James Bruchac. *The Girl Who Helped Thunder and Other Native American Folktales*. Sterling, 2008.

———. *When the Chenoo Howls: Native American Tales of Terror*. Walker, 1999.

Bruchac, Joseph, and Gayle Ross. *The Girl Who Married the Moon*. Bridge-Water, 1994.

Bryan, Ashley. *Ashley Bryan's African Tales, Uh-Huh*. Atheneum, 1998.

Burns, Batt. *The King with Horse's Ears and Other Irish Folktales*. Sterling, 2009.

Calvino, Italo. *Italian Folktales*. Mariner, 1992.

Casey, Dawn. *The Barefoot Book of Earth Tales*. Barefoot Books, 2009.

Chaikin, Miriam, ed. *Angel Secrets: Stories Based on Jewish Legend*. Henry Holt, 2006.

Chase, Richard. *Grandfather Tales*. Houghton Mifflin, 2003.

———. *Jack Tales*. Houghton Mifflin, 2003.

Chen, Haiyan, and Fang Li. *Eight Dragons on the Roof and Other Tales: Traditional Dragon Stories from China*. China Books, 2012.

Cheung, Shu Pei. *Walking on Solid Ground*. With Aaron Chau and Deborah Wei. Philadelphia Folklore Project, 2004.

Clarkson, Atelia, ed. *World Folktales: A Scribner Resource Collection*. Scribner, 1980.

Climo, Shirley. *Monkey Business: Stories from Around the World*. Henry Holt, 2005.

Conover, Sarah. *Ayat Jamilah (Beautiful Signs): A Treasury of Islamic Wisdom for Children and Parents*. Eastern Washington University Press, 2004.

———. *Kindness: A Treasury of Buddhist Wisdom for Children and Parents.* Eastern Washington University Press, 2001.

Courlander, Harold, and Wolf Leslau. *The Fire on the Mountain and Other Stories from Ethiopia and Eritrea.* Henry Holt, 1995.

Crossley-Holland, Kevin, ed. *Why the Fish Laughed and Other Tales.* Oxford University Press, 2002.

Daly, Ita. *Irish Myths and Legends.* Illus. by Bea Willey. Oxford University Press, 2001.

———. *Stories from Ireland.* Oxford University Press, 2009.

Dashdondog, Jamba. *Mongolian Folktales.* With Borolzoi Dashdondog. Libraries Unlimited, 2009.

DeArmond, Dal. *The Boy Who Found the Light.* Sierra, 1990.

De Barba Miller, Violet Teresa, ed. *Holiday Stories All Year Round: Audience Participation Stories and More.* Libraries Unlimited, 2008.

de Las Casas, Dianne. *Scared Silly: 25 Tales to Thrill Young Listeners.* Libraries Unlimited, 2010.

Dembicki, Matt. *Trickster: Native American Tales, a Graphic Collection.* Fulcrum Books, 2010.

Doucet, Sharon Arms. *Lapin Plays Possum: Trickster Tales from the Louisiana Bayou.* Farrar, Straus and Giroux, 2002.

Doyle, Malachy. *The Barefoot Book of Fairy Tales.* Barefoot Books, 2005.

———. *Tales from Old Ireland.* Illus. by Niamh Sharkey. Barefoot Books, 2000.

Duncan, Barbara R., ed. *The Origin of the Milky Way and Other Living Stories of the Cherokee.* University of North Carolina Press, 2008.

Dundas, Marjorie. *Riddling Tales from Around the World.* University Press of Mississippi, 2002.

Edgecomb, Diane. *A Fire in My Heart: Kurdish Tales.* With Mohammed M. A. Ahmed and Çeto Ozel. Libraries Unlimited, 2007.

Fang, Linda. *The Ch'i-lin Purse: A Collection of Ancient Chinese Stories.* Farrar, Straus and Giroux, 1995.

Feinstein, Edward M. *Capturing the Moon: Classic and Modern Jewish Tales*. Behrman House, 2008.

Fish, Andy. *Werewolves of Wisconsin and Other American Myths, Monsters and Ghosts*. McFarland, 2012.

Flood, Bo, Beret E. Strong, and William Flood. *Micronesian Legends*. Bess Press, 2002.

Ford, Lyn. *Affrilachian Folktales: Folktales from the African-American Appalachian Tradition*. Parkhurst Brothers, 2012.

Forest, Heather. *Wisdom Tales from Around the World*. August House, 1996.

———. *Wonder Tales from Around the World*. August House, 1997.

Friedman, Amy. *Tell Me a Story: Timeless Folktales from Around the World*. Friedman and Danziger, 2006.

Fujita, Hiroko. *Folktales from the Japanese Countryside*. Libraries Unlimited, 2007.

Gág, Wanda. *More Tales from Grimm*. Coward-McCann, 1947; University of Minnesota Press, 2006.

———. *Tales from Grimm*. Coward-McCann, 1936; University of Minnesota Press, 2006.

Galeano, Juan Carlos. *Folktales of the Amazon*. Libraries Unlimited, 2010.

Garcia, Emmett Shkeme. *Coyote and the Sky: How the Sun, Moon, and Stars Began*. University of New Mexico Press, 2006.

García, Nasario. *Brujerías: Stories of Witchcraft and the Supernatural in the American Southwest and Beyond*. Texas Tech University Press, 2007.

———. *Rattling Chains and Other Stories for Children/Ruido de cadenas y otros cuentos para niños*. Piñata Books, 2009.

Garner, Alan. *A Bag of Moonshine*. CollinsVoyager, 2002.

———. *Collected Folktales*. HarperCollins, 2011.

Gerson, Mary-Joan. *Fiesta Femenina: Celebrating Women in Mexican Folktale*. Illus. by Maya Christina Gonzalez. Barefoot Books, 2005.

Glass, Andrew. *Mountain Men: True Grit and Tall Tales*. Illus. by author. Doubleday, 2001.

Goble, Paul. *The Boy and His Mud Horses, and Other Tales from the Tipi.* World Wisdom, 2010.

González, Lucía M. *Señor Cat's Romance and Other Favorite Stories from Latin America.* Scholastic, 1997.

Greene, Ellin. *Midsummer Magic: A Garland of Stories, Charms, and Recipes.* Lothrop, 1977.

Grimm, Jacob, and Wilhelm Grimm. *About Wise Men and Simpletons.* Simon and Schuster, 1986.

———. *Household Stories of the Brothers Grimm.* Trans. by Lucy Crane. Dover, 1986.

———. *The Juniper Tree and Other Tales from Grimm.* Illus. by Maurice Sendak. Farrar, Straus and Giroux, 2003.

———. *McElderry Book of Grimms' Fairy Tales.* Adapted by Saviour Pirotta. McElderry, 2006.

Hamilton, Martha, and Mitch Weiss. *How and Why Stories: World Tales Kids Can Read and Tell.* August House, 1999.

———. *Scared Witless: Thirteen Eerie Tales to Tell.* August House, 2006.

———. *Through the Grapevine: World Tales Kids Can Read and Tell.* August House, 2001.

Hamilton, Mary. *Kentucky Folktales: Revealing Stories, Truths, and Outright Lies.* University Press of Kentucky, 2012.

Hamilton, Virginia. *The Dark Way: Stories from the Spirit World.* Harcourt Brace Jovanovich, 1990.

———. *Her Stories: African American Folktales, Fairy Tales, and True Tales.* Scholastic, 1995.

———. *Many Thousand Gone: African Americans from Slavery to Freedom.* Random House, 1993.

———. *The People Could Fly: American Black Folktales.* Knopf, 1992.

———. *Ring of Tricksters: Tales from America, West Indies and Africa.* Blue Sky, 1997.

———. *When Birds Could Talk and Bats Could Sing.* Blue Sky, 1996.

Harris, Christie. *Mouse Woman and the Mischief-Makers*. Raincoast Books, 2005.

Harris, Joel Chandler. *Jump! The Adventures of Brer Rabbit*. Adapted by Van Dyke Parks and Malcolm Jones. Harcourt, 1986.

———. *Jump Again! More Adventures of Brer Rabbit*. Adapted by Van Dyke Parks. Harcourt, 1987.

———. *Jump on Over! The Adventures of Brer Rabbit and His Family*. Adapted by Van Dyke Parks. Harcourt, 1989.

Hausman, Gerald, and Loretta Hausman. *Cats of Myth: Tales from Around the World*. Simon and Schuster, 2000.

Haviland, Virginia, ed. *Favorite Fairy Tales Told Around the World*. Little, Brown, 1985.

Hayes, Joe. *Dance, Nana, Dance / Baila, Nana, Baila: Cuban Folktales in English and Spanish*. Cinco Puntos Press, 2007.

He, Liyi. *The Spring of Butterflies and Other Folktales of China's Minority Peoples*. Lothrop, 1985.

Hearne, Betsy. *Beauties and Beasts*. Oryx, 1993.

Heins, Ethel. *The Cat and the Cook: And Other Fables of Krylov*. Greenwillow, 1995.

Hicks, Orville. *Jack Tales and Mountain Yarns as Told by Orville Hicks*. Transcription and text by Julia Taylor Ebel. Parkway, 2009.

Holt, David, and Bill Mooney, eds. *More Ready-to-Tell Tales from Around the World*. August House, 2000.

———. *Ready-to-Tell Tales*. August House, 1994.

Houston, James A. *James Houston's Treasury of Inuit Legends*. Harcourt, 2006.

Hume, Lotta Carswell. *Favorite Children's Stories from China and Tibet*. Tuttle, 1989.

Hurston, Zora Neale. *Every Tongue Got to Confess: Negro Folk-Tales from the Gulf States*. HarperCollins, 2001.

———. *Lies and Other Tall Tales*. Illus. by Christopher Myers. HarperCollins, 2005.

Ingham, Donna. *Tales with a Texas Twist: Original Stories and Enduring Folklore from the Lone Star State*. Globe Pequot, 2005.

Jacobs, Joseph. *English Fairy Tales*. David Nutt, 1890.

Jaffe, Nina. *Patakin: World Tales of Drums and Drummers*. Henry Holt, 1994.

———. *While Standing on One Foot: Puzzle Stories and Wisdom Tales from the Jewish Tradition*. Henry Holt, 1993.

Jamba, Dashdondog, and Borolzoi Dashdondong. *Mongolian Folktales*. Ed. by Anne Pellowski. Libraries Unlimited, 2009.

Jiang, Ji-Li. *The Magical Monkey King: Mischief in Heaven*. HarperCollins, 2002.

Johnson-Davies, Denys. *Goha the Wise Fool*. Philomel, 2005.

Keding, Dan. *Elder Tales: Stories of Wisdom and Courage from Around the World*. Libraries Unlimited, 2008.

———. *English Folktales*. Libraries Unlimited, 2005.

———. *Stories of Hope and Spirit*. August House, 2004.

———. *The United States of Storytelling: Folktales and True Stories from the Eastern States*. Libraries Unlimited, 2010.

———. *The United States of Storytelling: Folktales and True Tales from the Western States*. Libraries Unlimited, 2010.

Keens-Douglas, Richard. *Tales from the Island of Spice: A Collection of New Caribbean Folk Tales*. Annick, 2004.

Kimmel, Eric A. *The McElderry Book of Greek Myths*. Simon and Schuster Children's Publishing, 2008.

Kotarski, Georgiana C. *Ghosts of the Southern Tennessee Valley*. John F. Blair, 2006.

Krull, Kathleen. *A Pot o' Gold: A Treasury of Irish Stories, Poetry, Folklore, and (of course) Blarney*. Hyperion, 2004.

Laird, Elizabeth. *When the World Began*. Oxford University Press, 2000.

Lang, Andrew. *A World of Fairy Tales*. Dial, 1994.

Larson, Jean Russell. *The Fish Bride and Other Gypsy Tales*. Linnet Books, 2000.

Lattimore, Deborah Nourse. *Arabian Nights: Three Tales*. HarperCollins, 1995.

Leach, Maria. *Whistle in the Graveyard: Folk Tales to Chill Your Bones*. Puffin, 1982.

Lester, Julius. *Further Tales of Uncle Remus: The Misadventures of Brer Rabbit, Brer Fox, Brer Wolf, the Doodang, and Other Creatures*. Illus. by Jerry Pinkney. Dial, 1989.

———. *How Many Spots Does a Leopard Have? And Other Tales*. Scholastic, 1989.

———. *The Knee-High Man and Other Tales*. Dial, 1972, 1985.

———. *The Last Tales of Uncle Remus*. Dial, 1994.

———. *More Tales of Uncle Remus: Further Adventures of Brer Rabbit, His Friends, Enemies, and Others*. Dial, 1988.

———. *The Tales of Uncle Remus: The Adventures of Brer Rabbit*. Dial, 1987.

Livo, Norma J., ed. *Moon Cakes to Maize: Delicious World Folktales*. Fulcrum Resources, 1999.

———. *Story Medicine: Multicultural Tales of Healing and Transformation*. Libraries Unlimited, 2001.

———. *Tales to Tickle Your Funny Bone: Humorous Tales from Around the World*. Libraries Unlimited, 2007.

———. *Troubadour's Storybag: Musical Folktales of the World*. Fulcrum Books, 1996.

Livo, Norma J., and Dia Cha. *Folk Stories of the Hmong: Peoples of Laos, Thailand, and Vietnam*. Libraries Unlimited, 1991.

Livo, Norma J., and George O. Livo. *The Enchanted Wood and Other Tales from Finland*. Libraries Unlimited, 1999.

Lundburgh, Holger. *Swedish Folk Tales*. Floris, 2004.

Lunge-Larsen, Lise. *The Hidden Folk: Stories of Fairies, Dwarves, Selkies, and Other Secret Beings*. Houghton Mifflin, 2004.

———. *The Troll with No Heart in His Body and Other Tales of Trolls from Norway*. Houghton Mifflin, 1999.

Lupton, Hugh. *Riddle Me This! Riddles and Stories to Challenge Your Mind.* Barefoot Books, 2003.

———. *Tales of Mystery and Magic.* Barefoot Books, 2010.

Lurie, Alison. *Clever Gretchen and Other Forgotten Folktales.* Crowell, 1980.

MacDonald, Margaret Read. *Shake-It-Up Tales! Stories to Sing, Dance, Drum, and Act Out.* August House, 2000.

———. *The Singing Top: Tales from Malaysia, Singapore, and Brunei.* Libraries Unlimited, 2008.

———. *Tom Thumb: The Oryx Multicultural Folktale Series.* Oryx, 1993.

———. *Twenty Tellable Tales: Audience Participation Folktales for the Beginning Storyteller.* American Library Association, 2004.

———. *When the Lights Go Out: Twenty Scary Tales to Tell.* H. W. Wilson, 1988.

MacManus, Seumas. *Donegal Fairy Stories.* Dover, 1968.

———. *Hibernian Nights.* Barnes and Noble Books, 1994.

Malinowski, Michal, and Anne Pellowski. *Polish Folktales and Folklore.* Libraries Unlimited, 2009.

Mama, Raouf. *Why Monkeys Live in Trees and Other Stories from Benin.* Curbstone, 2006.

Manitonquat (Medicine Story). *The Children of the Morning Light: Wampanoag Tales.* Macmillan, 1994.

Martin, Rafe. *Endless Path: Jataka Tales with Commentaries.* North Atlantic Books, 2010.

———. *The Hungry Tigress: Buddhist Legends and Jataka Tales.* Parallax, 1990.

———. *Mysterious Tales of Japan.* Illus. by Tatsuro Kiuchi. Putnam, 1993.

Matthews, Caitlin. *Fireside Stories for a Winter's Eve.* Barefoot Books, 2007.

Matthews, John. *Trick of the Tale: A Collection of Trickster Tales.* Candlewick, 2008.

McCaughrean, Geraldine. *One Thousand and One Arabian Nights.* Oxford University Press, 1999.

McGill, Alice. *Sure as Sunrise: Stories of Bruh Rabbit and His Walkin' Talkin' Friends*. Houghton, 2004.

McIntosh, Gavin. *Hausaland Tales from the Nigerian Marketplace*. Linnet Books/ShoeString, 2002.

McKissack, Patricia C. *Porch Lies: Tales of Slicksters, Tricksters, and Other Wily Characters*. Illus. by André Carrilho. Schwartz and Wade, 2006.

McNeil, Heather. *The Celtic Breeze: Stories of the Otherworld from Scotland, Ireland, and Wales*. Libraries Unlimited, 2001.

Medearis, Angela Shelf. *Haunts: Five Hair-Raising Tales*. Holiday House, 1996.

Minard, Rosemary. *Womenfolk and Fairy Tales*. Houghton Mifflin, 1975.

Molner, Irma. *One Time Dog Market at Buda and Other Hungarian Folktales*. Illus. by Georgeta-Elena Enesel. Linnet Books, 2001.

Nic Leodhas, Sorche. *Heather and Broom: Tales of the Scottish Highlands*. Henry Holt, 1960.

———. *Sea Spell and Moor Magic*. Holt, Rinehart and Winston, 1968.

———. *Twelve Great Black Cats*. Dutton, 1973.

Norman, Howard. *The Girl Who Dreamed Only Geese and Other Tales of the Far North*. Harcourt, 1997.

———. *How Glooskap Outwits the Ice Giants*. Little, Brown, 1989.

———. *Trickster and the Fainting Birds*. Illus. by Tom Pohrt. Harcourt, 1999.

Nuweihed, Jamal Sleem. *Abu Jmeel's Daughter and Other Stories: Arab Folk Tales from Palestine and Lebanon*. Interlink, 2002.

Oberman, Sheldon. *Solomon and the Ant and Other Jewish Folktales*. Boyds Mills, 2006.

Olson, Arielle North. *Ask the Bones: Scary Stories from Around the World*. With Howard Schwartz. Puffin, 2002.

———. *More Bones: Scary Stories from Around the World*. With Howard Schwartz. Viking, 2008.

Palmer, Michele. *Ghosts and Golems*. Jewish Publication Society, 2001.

Parkhurst, Liz, ed. *The August House Book of Scary Stories: Spooky Stories for Telling Out Loud*. August House, 2009.

Pellowski, Anne. *Drawing Stories from Around the World and a Sampling of European Handkerchief Stories*. Libraries Unlimited, 2005.

Pérez, Elvia. *From the Winds of Manguito: Cuban Folktales in English and Spanish*. Libraries Unlimited, 2004.

———. *Fairy Tales from Eastern Europe*. Illus. by Larry Wilkes. Houghton Mifflin, 1991.

Phelps, Ethel Johnston. *Maid of the North*. Henry Holt, 1981.

Philip, Neil. *Horse Hooves and Chicken Feet: Mexican Folktales*. Clarion, 2003.

———. *Stockings of Buttermilk: American Folktales*. Text by Neil Philip. Illus. by Jacqueline Mair. Clarion, 1999.

Power, Effie. *Bag o' Tales: A Sourcebook for Storytellers*. Dutton, 1934; Dover, 1970.

Ragan, Kathleen, ed. *Fearless Girls, Wise Women, and Beloved Sisters: Heroines in Folktales from Around the World*. Norton, 1997.

———. *Outfoxing Fear: Folktales from Around the World*. Norton, 2006.

Ramujan, Raik. *Folktales from India*. Pantheon, 1994.

Ransome, Arthur. *Old Peter's Russian Tales*. Viking, 1975.

Reneaux, J. J. *Cajun Folktales*. August House, 1992.

———. *Haunted Bayou and Other Cajun Ghost Stories*. August House, 1994.

———. *How Animals Saved the People: Animal Tales from the South*. HarperCollins, 2001.

Riordan, James. *The Woman in the Moon and Other Tales of Forgotten Heroines*. Dial, 1985.

Rockwell, Anne. *The Old Woman and Her Pig*. Crowell, 1979.

———. *The Three Bears and Fifteen Other Stories*. Crowell, 1979.

Ross, Gayle. *How Rabbit Tricked Otter and Other Cherokee Trickster Stories*. HarperCollins, 1994.

Roth, Rita. *The Power of Song and Other Sephardic Tales*. Jewish Publication Society, 2007.

Running Wolf, Michael. *On the Trail of Elder Brother*. Persea, 2000.

Ryan, Patrick. *Shakespeare's Storybook: Folk Tales that Inspired the Bard*. Barefoot Books, 2002.

San Souci, Robert D. *Short and Shivery: Thirty Chilling Tales*. Doubleday, 1987. (See also: *More Short and Shivery*; *Even More Short and Shivery*; *A Terrifying Taste of Short and Shivery*.)

————. *Sister Tricksters: Rollicking Tales of Clever Females*. LittleFolk, 2006.

Schram, Peninnah. *The Hungry Clothes and Other Jewish Folktales*. Sterling, 2008.

Schwartz, Alvin. *Scary Stories to Tell in the Dark*. Harper, 1986.

Schwartz, Howard. *The Day the Rabbi Disappeared: Jewish Holiday Tales of Magic*. Viking, 2000.

————. *Elijah's Violin and Other Jewish Fairy Tales*. Illus. by Linda Heller. Oxford University Press, 1994.

————. *Kingdoms: Jewish Tales of Angels, Spirits, and Demons*. Harper-Collins, 2002.

Serwadda, W. Moses. *Songs and Stories from Uganda*. World Music Press, 1987.

Shannon, George. *More Stories to Solve*. Greenwillow, 1991.

————. *Still More Stories to Solve: Fourteen Folktales from Around the World*. Greenwillow, 1994.

————. *Stories to Solve: Folktales from Around the World*. Greenwillow, 1985.

Shelby, Anne. *The Adventures of Molly Whuppie and Other Appalachian Folktales*. University of North Carolina Press, 2007.

Sherlock, Philip M. *West Indian Folk Tales*. Oxford University Press, 1988.

Sherman, Josepha. *Trickster Tales*. August House, 1996.

Sierra, Judy. *Can You Guess My Name? Traditional Tales Around the World*. Clarion, 2002.

————. *Nursery Tales Around the World*. Clarion, 1996.

Singer, Isaac B. *The Fools of Chelm and Their History*. Farrar, Straus and Giroux, 1973.

————. *When Shlemiel Went to Warsaw and Other Stories*. Farrar, Straus and Giroux, 1992.

Song, Tamarack, and Moses Amik Beaver. *Whispers of the Ancients: Native Tales for Teaching and Healing in Our Time*. University of Michigan Press, 2010.

Spencer, Ann. *Song of the Sea: Myths, Tales and Folklore*. Tundra, 2001.

Stoutenburg, Adrien. *American Tall Tales*. Puffin, 1976.

Strauss, Kevin. *Tales with Tails: Storytelling the Wonders of the Natural World*. Libraries Unlimited, 2006.

Sugiura, Kuniko. *Indonesian Fables of Feats and Fortunes*. Heian International, 2007.

————. *Indonesian Tales of Treasures and Brides*. Heian International, 2007.

Taback, Simms. *Kibitzers and Fools: Tales My Zayda Told Me*. Viking, 2005.

Tatar, Maria. *The Annotated Classic Fairy Tales*. Norton, 2002.

Taylor, C. J. *Spirits, Fairies, and Merpeople*. Tundra Books, 2009.

Tchana, Katrin. *Changing Woman and Her Sisters: Stories of Goddesses from Around the World*. Holiday House, 2006.

————. *The Serpent Slayer and Other Tales of Strong Women*. Little, Brown, 2000.

Thompson, M. Terry. *Salish Myths and Legends: One People's Stories*. With Steven M. Egesdal. University of Nebraska Press, 2008.

Thompson, Susan Conklin, and others. *Mayan Folktales / Cuentos folklóricos mayas*. Libraries Unlimited, 2007.

Tingle, Tim. *Spirits Dark and Light: Supernatural Tales from the Five Civilized Tribes*. August House, 2006.

Tingle, Tim, and Doc Moore. *More Spooky Texas Tales: The "Shriekquel" to an Earlier Collection of Ghost Stories*. Texas Tech University Press, 2010.

Tossa, Wajuppa. *Lao Folktales*. Libraries Unlimited, 2008.

Townsend, John. *Mysterious Urban Myths*. Raintree, 2004.

Tucker, Elizabeth. *Campus Legends: A Handbook*. Greenwood, 2005.

Vigil, Angel. *The Eagle on the Cactus: Traditional Stories from Mexico*. Libraries Unlimited, 2000.

Vittorini, Domenico. *Thread of Life: Twelve Old Italian Tales*. Knopf, 1995.

Vuong, Lynette Dyer. *The Brocaded Slipper and Other Vietnamese Tales*. Harper, 1992.

———. *The Golden Carp: And Other Tales from Vietnam*. Lothrop, 1993.

Walker, Barbara K. *The Dancing Palm Tree and Other Nigerian Folktales*. Texas Tech University Press, 1990.

———. *A Treasury of Turkish Folktales for Children*. Linnet Books, 1998.

———. *Watermelons, Walnuts, and the Wisdom of Allah and Other Tales of the Hoca*. With Harold Berson. Texas Tech University Press, 1991.

Walker, Paul Robert. *Giants!* Harcourt, 1995.

Walker, Richard. *The Barefoot Book of Pirates*. Barefoot Books, 1998.

Washington, Donna. *A Pride of African Tales*. HarperCollins, 2004.

Webster, M. L. *On the Trail Made of Dawn: Native American Creation Stories*. Linnet Books, 2001.

Williams, Marcia. *The Elephant's Friend and Other Tales from Ancient India*. Candlewick, 2012.

Williamson, Duncan. *The Broonie, Silkies and Fairies: Travellers' Tales of the Other World*. Harmony, 1987.

———. *Fireside Tales of the Traveller Children*. Harmony Books, 1983.

———. *Tales of the Seal People: Scottish Folk Tales*. Interlink, 1998.

Wilson, Barbara Ker. *Stories from Scotland*. Oxford University Press, 2009.

Wolkstein, Diane. *The Magic Orange Tree and Other Haitian Folktales*. Schocken Books, 1987.

———. *Treasures of the Heart: Holiday Stories That Reveal the Soul of Judaism*. Schocken Books, 2003.

Wood, Ramsay. *Kalila and Dimna: Fables of Friendship and Betrayal*. Saqi Books, 2008.

Yeats, W. B. *Fairy Tales of Ireland.* Delacorte, 1990.

Yellow Robe, Rosebud. *Tonweya and the Eagles and Other Lakota Tales.* Dial, 1992.

Yep, Laurence. *The Rainbow People.* HarperCollins, 1989.

————. *Tongues of Jade.* HarperCollins, 1991.

Yolen, Jane. *Favorite Folktales from Around the World.* Pantheon, 1988.

————. *Mightier Than the Sword: World Folktales for Strong Boys.* Silver Whistle, 2003.

————. *Not One Damsel in Distress: World Folktales for Strong Girls.* Silver Whistle, 2000.

Yuan, Haiwang. *Princess Peacock: Tales from the Other Peoples of China.* Libraries Unlimited, 2008.

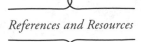
STORIES AND STORYTELLING
ON THE WEB

This is far from a complete list of available Web resources; rather, it is a selection of particularly useful sites when searching for folktales, information on folktales, or information on storytelling and storytelling groups and organizations. In addition to the sites noted, there are a growing number of digital collections containing public domain resources. Many countries, regions, and states have storytelling groups and organizations; just a token few are noted here.

Aaron Shepard's Storytelling Page, www.aaronshep.com/storytelling/index
.html

American Folklore, www.americanfolklore.net

American Indians in Children's Literature, http://americanindiansin
childrensliterature.blogspot.com

Andrew Lang's Fairy Books, www.mythfolklore.net/andrewlang

Australian Storytelling, www.australianstorytelling.org.au

Baldwin Online Children's Literature Project, www.mainlesson.com/main /displayarticle.php?article=feature

Cabinet des Fées, www.cabinetdesfees.com

Center for Digital Storytelling, www.storycenter.org

Circle of Stories, www.pbs.org/circleofstories

Connecticut Storytelling Center, www.connstorycenter.org

Encyclopedia Mythica, www.pantheon.org

Fairy Tale Review, http://digitalcommons.wayne.edu/fairytalereview

Folk and Fairy Tales, www.pitt.edu/~dash/ashliman.html

Folklinks, www.pitt.edu/~dash/folklinks.html

Folklore and Mythology, www.pitt.edu/~dash/folktexts.html

Folktales, www.indiana.edu/~afrist/outreach/teaching.shtml

Folktales from Many Lands, http://digital.library.upenn.edu/women/gask /tales/tales.html

Folktales.net, www.folktales.net

Folktexts (Folklore and Mythology Electronic Texts), www.pitt.edu/~dash /folktexts2.html

Google Books, books.google.com (search for "folktales" or "fairy tales" and click on free e-books link for public domain materials)

Illinois Storytelling, Inc., www.storytelling.org

International School of Storytelling, www.schoolofstorytelling.com

Internet Sacred Text Archive, www.sacred-texts.com

Internet Storytelling Center and Bookstore, www.story-telling.com

Karen Chace, Professional Storyteller and Web Researcher, www.storybug .net

League for the Advancement of New England Storytelling, www.lanes.org

Library of Congress American Folklife Center, www.loc.gov/folklife

Marvels and Tales, http://digitalcommons.wayne.edu/marvels

National Council of Teachers of English Position Paper on Storytelling, www.ncte.org/positions/statements/teachingstorytelling

National Storytelling Network, www.storynet.org

Northlands Storytelling Network, www.northlands.net

Oral Tradition Journal, http://journal.oraltradition.org

Parabola, www.parabola.org

Project Gutenberg, www.gutenberg.org

Snopes.com (Urban Legends Reference Pages), www.snopes2.com

Sources for the Analysis and Interpretation of Folk and Fairy Tales, www.folkandfairy.org/index.html#LIST

StoryArts Online, www.storyarts.org

Story Lover's World, www.story-lovers.com

Storytell Listserv, www.storynet.org/storytell.html

Storyteller.net, www.storyteller.net

Storytelling!, www.planetesme.com/storytelling.html

Storytelling Center of New York City, www.storytelling-nyc.org

Storytelling Magazine, www.storynet.org/magazine.html

Storytelling, Self, Society, www.tandfonline.com/toc/hsts20/current

SurLaLuneFairytales.com, www.surlalunefairytales.com

Tell Me a Story, www.web.net/~story/mbstory.htm

Tim Sheppard's Storytelling Resources for Storytellers, www.timsheppard .co.uk/story

Youth Storytelling, www.youthstorytelling.com

INDEX

A

About Wise Men and Simpletons: Twelve Tales from the Brothers Grimm (Shub), 80

About Wise Men and Simpletons (Grimm Brothers), 42

Ada, Alma Flor, 152, 154

Aesop, 32, 35, 36, 41–42

Aesop's Fables (Pinkney), 41

Aesop's Fables (Sneed), 35, 41

Afanasyev, Alexander, 19

age groupings for storytelling events, list of, 5

ages 3 to 6

    Chicken Little (Emberley and Emberley), 18

    The Enormous Potato (Davis), 18

    Flannel Board Storytelling Book (Sierra), 10

    The Giant Carrot (Peck), 18

    The Gigantic Turnip (Tolstoy), 18

    Go to Sleep, Gecko! A Balinese Folktale (MacDonald), 18

    Grandma Lena's Big Ol' Turnip (Hester), 18

    The Great Big Enormous Turnip (retold by Janice M. Del Negro for this book), 19–21

    The Hungry Wolf (retold by Janice M. Del Negro for this book), 21–24

    The Lion and the Mouse (Pinkney), 18

    A Little Story about a Big Turnip (Zunshine), 18

    Mrs. Chicken and the Hungry Crocodile (Paye), 18

    Multicultural Folktales: Stories to Tell Young Children, 10

    Nursery Tales Around the World (Sierra), 18

    overview, 9–12

    participatory element, stories with, 10–12

ages 3 to 6 *(continued)*
play, learning through, 9–10
PLOP! Splash! A Folktale from Tibet
(retold by Janice M. Del Negro
for this book), 27–30
The Red Hen (Emberley and
Emberley), 18
resources for storyteller and
suggested readings, 17–18
The Teeny-Tiny Woman (retold by
Janice M. Del Negro for this
book), 25–26
"The Three Billy Goats Gruff" -
storycoaching example, 12–17
The Three Billy Goats Gruff (Dewan),
18
The Three Billy Goats Gruff
(Galdone), 18
*The Three Billy Goats Gruff/Los Tres
Chivitos* (Ottolenghi), 18
The Three Billy Goats Gruff (Stevens),
18
*What! Cried Granny: An Almost
Bedtime Story; A Silly, Funny
Granny Tries to Put Her
Grandson to Bed* (Lum), 18
Yummy: Eight Favorite Fairy Tales
(Cousins), 17
ages 6 to 9
About Wise Men and Simpletons
(Grimm Brothers), 42
Aesop's Fables (Pinkney), 41
Aesop's Fables (Sneed), 41
Ashley Bryan's African Tales, Uh-Huh
(Bryan), 42
Big Scary House (Washington), 43
The Boy Who Cried Wolf (Hennessy),
41
Buddha Stories (Demi), 42
*The Contest between the Sun and the
Wind* (Forest), 42
creative dramatics, 33–34
*The Day It Snowed Tortillas/El dia que
nevaron tortillas* (Hayes), 42
Fairly Fairy Tales (Codell), 42

*Favorite Fairy Tales Told Around the
World* (Haviland), 42
Fox Tails: Four Fables from Aesop
(Lowry), 43
The Giant and the Beanstalk
(Stanley), 43
The Great Race (O'Malley), 43
*The Hare and the Tortoise and Other
Fables of La Fontaine* (La
Fontaine), 43
The Hedley Kow (retold by Janice M.
Del Negro for this book), 44–48
*I Once Was a Monkey: Stories Buddha
Told* (Lee), 43
Jack and His Comrades (retold by
Janice M. Del Negro for this
book), 48–56
*Jack and the Beanstalk: The Graphic
Novel* (Hoena), 42
Jack and the Beanstalk (Walker), 43
King Hairy Goat Ears (retold by
Janice M. Del Negro for this
book), 56–60
length of stories, 34–35
The Lion and the Mouse (Pinkney),
42
literacy skills, acquiring, 33
Lousy Rotten Stinkin' Grapes
(Palatini), 43
*The Magic Orange Tree and Other
Haitian Folktales* (Wolkstein),
43
The Magic Porridge Pot (Galdone), 42
The Monkey, the Dog, and the Carabao
(retold by Janice M. Del Negro
for this book), 61–65
More Tales from Grimm (Grimm
Brothers), 42
The North Wind and the Sun: A Fable
(La Fontaine), 43
"The North Wind and the Sun" -
storycoaching example, 36–41
overview, 31–35
participatory element, stories with,
32

ages 6 to 9 *(continued)*
    Rapunzel (Gibb), 42
    resources for storyteller and
        suggested readings, 41–43
    A Sip of Aesop (Yolen), 43
    Soap! Soap! Soap! Don't Forget the
        Soap! An Appalachian Folktale
        (Birdseye), 42
    Stone Soup (Brown), 42
    Stone Soup (McGovern), 43
    Stone Soup (Muth), 43
    Tales from Grimm (Grimm Brothers),
        42
    The Uglified Ducky (Claflin), 42
    Unwitting Wisdom: An Anthology of
        Aesop's Fables (Ward), 43
    Very Short Fables to Read Together
        (Hoberman), 42
    Wiley and the Hairy Man (Sierra), 43
    The Wind and the Sun (Hawes), 42
ages 9 to 12
    audience participation, 69
    A Big Spooky House! (Washington), 81
    The Big Toe: An Appalachian Ghost
        Story (Kirby), 81
    "Chunk o' Meat" (*Grandfather Tales*),
        80
    creative dramatics, 67
    Definitely Not for Little Ones: Very
        Grimm Fairy-Tale Comics
        (Berner), 80
    The Demon Goblin of Adachigahara
        (retold by Janice M. Del Negro
        for this book), 89–94
    Even Higher (Ungar), 81
    Finn McCool and the Great Fish: A
        Story about Acquiring Wisdom
        (Bunting), 80
    Four Friends and a Lion (retold by
        Janice M. Del Negro for this
        book), 82–85
    The Ghost Catcher: A Bengali Folktale
        (Hamilton and Weiss), 80
    The Goat-Faced Girl: A Classic Italian
        Folktale (Sharpe), 81

"The Golden Goose" (Grimm
    Brothers), abbreviated version
    of, 70–72
Joe Cinders (Mitchell), 81
learning stories, 69
length of stories, 68
Liver (retold by Janice M. Del Negro
    for this book), 85–89
"My Big Toe" (*Diane Goode's Book of*
    Scary Stories and Songs), 81
overview, 67–70
Pigling: A Cinderella Story: A Korean
    Tale (Jolley), 80
The Race of the Birkebeiners (Lunge-
    Larsen), 81
resources for storyteller and
    suggested readings, 80–81
structure of effective oral story,
    70–73
supernatural or gory story, 73
Tailypo: A Newfangled Tall Tale
    (Medearis), 81
"Tailypo, a Jump Tale" -
    storycoaching example, 73–80
"Tailypo" (Torrence), 81
Tailypo! (Wahl), 81
The Tailypo: A Ghost Story (Galdone),
    80
"The Big Hairy Tale" (*Jackie Tales*),
    80
"The Golden Goose" (*About Wise*
    Men and Simpletons: Twelve Tales
    from the Brothers Grimm), 80
"The Peculiar Such Thing" (*The*
    People Could Fly: American Black
    Folktales), 81
There's a Princess in the Palace (Alley),
    80
Tsunami! (Kajikawa), 80
Velcome (O'Malley), 81
To Your Good Health! (retold by
    Janice M. Del Negro for this
    book), 94–102
ages 12 to 14
    The Arabian Nights (Tarnowska), 115

ages 12 to 14 *(continued)*
    Calamity Jack (Hale), 114
    Clever Grethel (retold by Janice
        M. Del Negro for this book),
        122–125
    Cloaked in Red (Vande Velde), 115
    The Crane Wife (Bodkin), 114
    "Cupid and Psyche" (*Greek Myths*),
        114
    *The Exploding Toilet: Modern Urban
        Legends* (Holt and Mooney),
        114
    "The Fire on the Mountain" (*The
        Fire on the Mountain and
        Other Stories from Ethiopia and
        Eritrea*), 114
    Fractured Fables (Valentino and
        Simon), 115
    A Ghost Story (retold by Janice M.
        Del Negro for this book),
        116–121
    Gilgamesh the Hero (McCaughrean),
        115
    "Godfather Death" (*Grimms' Tales
        for Young and Old: The Complete
        Stories*), 114
    humor in stories, 105
    "Keewahkee" (*When the Chenoo
        Howls: Native American Tales of
        Terror*), 114
    "La Muerta: Godmother Death"
        (*Ready-to-Tell Tales*), 114
    loyalty and friendship in stories, 105
    The Magic Pipe: A Norse Tale (retold
        by Janice M. Del Negro for this
        book), 126–139
    "Mary Culhane and the Dead Man"
        (*Goblin's Giggles and Other
        Stories*), 114
    "Mr. Fox" - storycoaching example,
        107–113
    "Nesoowa and the Chenoo" (*The
        Serpent Slayer and Other Stories
        of Strong Women*), 115

    overview, 103–107
    "Pygmalion and Galatea"
        (*Mythology*), 115
    *Rabbi Harvey vs. the Wisdom Kid:
        A Graphic Novel of Dueling
        Jewish Folktales in the Wild West*
        (Sheinkin), 115
    Rapunzel's Revenge (Hale), 114
    *Red Ridin' in the Hood and Other
        Cuentos* (Marcantonio), 114
    resources for storyteller and
        suggested readings, 114–115
    romantic stories, 104
    "The Sea Captain's Wife" (*Twelve
        Great Black Cats and Other Eerie
        Scottish Tales*), 115
    *Spiders in the Hairdo: Modern Urban
        Legends* (Holt and Mooney),
        114
    straightforward presentation, 106
    "Strength" (*Peace Tales*), 115
    supernatural or gory story, 106–107
    *Sword of the Samurai: Adventure
        Stories from Japan* (Kimmel),
        114
    "The Three Young Men and Death"
        (*Medieval Tales*), 115
    *Trickster: Native American Tales, a
        Graphic Collection* (Dembicki),
        114
    The Wild Geese (retold by Janice
        M. Del Negro for this book),
        140–147
Alley, Zoe B., 80
American Folk-Lore Journal, 48
American Library Association, 149
The Arabian Nights (Tarnowska),
    115
Asbjørnsen, Peter Christen, 12
Ashley Bryan's African Tales, Uh-Huh
    (Bryan), 34, 42
Ashliman, D. L., 85
audience participation, 69
authenticity of folktales, 152–153

B

Baker, Augusta, 152, 154

*A Baker's Dozen: Thirteen Stories to Tell
and Read Aloud* (Davis), 155

Bang, Molly, 107, 114

beginning storytelling books
    Cupid and Psyche (Craft), 7
    The Gingerbread Boy (Cook), 7
    The Great Big Enormous Turnip
        (Tolstoi), 8
    Little Red Riding Hood (Marshall), 8
    *Putting the World in a Nutshell:
        The Art of the Forumula Tale*
        (Dailey), 7
    *The Serpent Slayer and Other Stories of
        Strong Women* (Tchana), 8
    *The Storyteller's Start-Up Book:
        Finding, Learning, Performing
        and Using Folktales*
        (MacDonald), 8
    Storytelling: Art and Technique
        (Greene and Del Negro), 8
    *The Storytelling Classroom:
        Applications across the
        Curriculum* (Norfolk, Stenson,
        and Williams), 8
    The Three Billy Goats Gruff
        (Galdone), 8
    *Trickster: Native American Tales, a
        Graphic Collection* (Dembicki),
        8
    *Twenty Tellable Tales: Audience
        Participation Folktales for the
        Beginning Storyteller* (American
        Library Association), 8
    The Way of the Storyteller (Sawyer), 8

Bergen, Fannie D., 48

Berner, Rotraut Susanne, 80

Big Scary House (Washington), 43

A Big Spooky House! (Washington), 81

"The Big Hairy Tale" (*Jackie Tales*), 80

The Big Toe: An Appalachian Ghost Story
    (Kirby), 81

Birch, Carol, 70, 151

Birdseye, Tom, 42

Bodkin, Odds, 114

"The Bones of Story" (*Horn Book
    Magazine*), 155

The Boy Who Cried Wolf (Hennessy), 41

"The Bremen Town Musicians," 48

*The Broken Flute: The Native Experience
    in Books for Children* (Seale and
    Slapin), 156

Brothers Grimm, 34

Brown, Marcia, 42

Bruchac, James, 114

Bruchac, Joseph, 114

Bryan, Ashley, 42

Buddha Stories (Demi), 42

Bunting, Eve, 80

C

Cai, Mingshui, 155

Calamity Jack (Hale), 114

Caldwell, Eleanor H., 82

*Can You Guess My Name: Traditional Tales
    Around the World* (Sierra), 156

Chase, Richard, 48, 80

Chasse, Emily S., 155

Chicago Public Library, 1

Chicken Little (Emberley and Emberley),
    18

"Chunk o' Meat" (*Grandfather Tales*), 80

"Cite the Source: Reducing Cultural
    Chaos in Picture Books, Part
    One" (*School Library Journal*),
    155

Claflin, Willy, 42

"Clever Grethel" (Brothers Grimm), 105

Clever Grethel (retold by Janice M. Del
    Negro for this book), 122–125

climax of story, 72

"Clinkety-Clink" (*More Scary Stories to
    Tell in the Dark*), 116

Cloaked in Red (Vande Velde), 115

Codell, Esme Raji, 42

collections, folktale, 179–194

conclusions of stories, 72

The Contest between the Sun and the Wind (Forest), 35, 42
Cook, Scott, 6, 7
Coolidge, Olivia E., 114
copyright issues, 7
A Corpse Claims Its Property (website), 85
Courlander, Harold, 114
Cousins, Lucy, 17
Cowell, E. B., 27
Craft, K. Y., 6, 7
Crane, Lucy, 122
"The Crane Wife," 105
The Crane Wife (Bodkin), 114
creative dramatics
    ages 6 to 9, 33–34
    ages 9 to 12, 67
    overview, 3
crediting author for folktales, 152
The Crimson Fairy Book (Lang), 94
Cunliffe, John William, 82
Cupid and Psyche (Craft), 6, 7, 105
"Cupid and Psyche" (*Greek Myths*), 114
current state of storytelling, 149–154

D
Dailey, Sheila, 5, 7
"Damon and Pythias," 68
Dasent, George Webbe, 12
Davis, Aubrey, 18
Davis, Mary Gould, 152, 155
The Day It Snowed Tortillas/El día que nevaron tortillas (Hayes), 42
Dean, Ted, 18
Definitely Not for Little Ones: Very Grimm Fairy-Tale Comics (Berner), 80
Del Negro, Janice M., 8, 12, 19, 151. *See also* stories retold by Janice M. Del Negro for this book
Dembicki, Matt, 6, 8, 114
Demi, 42
The Demon Goblin of Adachigahara (retold by Janice M. Del Negro for this book), 89–94

Dewan, Ted, 18
"Die kleine Geschichte" (*Ostmäkische Sagen, Märchen und Erzälunge*), 85
Dominican University, 5

E
Earth Care: World Folktales to Talk About (MacDonald), 156
"East o' the Sun and West o' the Moon," 104
educational benefits of storytelling, 150
Emberley, Ed, 18
Emberley, Rebecca, 18
Emerson, Laura S., 106
English Fairy Tales (Jacobs), 107
The Enormous Potato (Davis), 18
Entertainer and Entertained (Caldwell), 82
Evans, Dorothy, 1
Even Higher (Ungar), 81
The Exploding Toilet: Modern Urban Legends (Holt and Mooney), 114

F
Fairly Fairy Tales (Codell), 42
Fairy Tales and Feminism: New Approaches (Haase), 155
Fansler, Dean S., 61
Favorite Fairy Tales Told Around the World (Haviland), 42, 155
Favorite Fairy Tales Told in Russia (Haviland), 94
Filipino Popular Tales (Fansler), 61
Finn McCool and the Great Fish: A Story about Acquiring Wisdom (Bunting), 80
The Fire on the Mountain and Other Stories from Ethiopia and Eritrea (Courlander and Leslau), 114
"The Fire on the Mountain" (*The Fire on the Mountain and Other Stories from Ethiopia and Eritrea*), 114
Flannel Board Storytelling Book (Sierra), 10

Flossie and the Fox (McKissack), 21
Folk Tales from China (Foreign Languages
  Press), 27
folktales. *See also* suggested readings
  authenticity of, 152–153
  collections of, 179–194
  crediting author for, 152
  negative views of, 152
  overview, 4–5
  picture books, 165–177
  positive views of, 152
  resources for researching, 157–159
  Web resources, 195–197
Forest, Heather, 35, 42, 152, 155
Four Friends and a Lion (retold by Janice
  M. Del Negro for this book),
  82–85
Fox Tails: Four Fables from Aesop (Lowry),
  43
Fractured Fables (Valentino and Simon),
  115
friendship and loyalty in stories, 105
"From Me to You" (*Summoned by Books:
  Essays and Speeches*), 9
Fu, Shelley, 152, 155

G

Galdone, Joanna, 80
Galdone, Paul, 2, 8, 12, 18, 32, 42
A Ghost Story (retold by Janice M. Del
  Negro for this book), 116–121
The Ghost Catcher: A Bengali Folktale
  (Hamilton and Weiss), 80
The Giant and the Beanstalk (Stanley), 43
The Giant Carrot (Peck), 18
Gibb, Sarah, 42
The Gigantic Turnip (Tolstoy), 18
Gilgamesh the Hero (McCaughrean),
  115
The Gingerbread Boy (Cook), 6, 7, 9
Go to Sleep, Gecko! A Balinese Folktale
  (MacDonald), 18
*The Goat-Faced Girl: A Classic Italian
  Folktale* (Sharpe), 81

"The Goat's Ears of the Emperor Trojan"
  (*The Violet Fairy Book*), 56
Goblin's Giggles and Other Stories (Bang),
  107, 114
"Godfather Death" (*Grimms' Tales for
  Young and Old: The Complete
  Stories*), 114
"The Golden Goose" (*About Wise Men
  and Simpletons: Twelve Tales from
  the Brothers Grimm*), 80
"The Golden Goose" (Grimm Brothers),
  70
"The Golden Goose" (Grimm Brothers),
  abbreviated version of, 70–72
The Golden Lynx and Other Tales (Baker),
  154
gory or supernatural story
  ages 9 to 12, 73
  ages 12 to 14, 106–107
Graduate School of Library and
  Information Science at
  Dominican University, 5
Grandfather Tales (Chase), 80
Grandma Lena's Big Ol' Turnip (Hester),
  18
The Great Big Enormous Turnip (retold by
  Janice M. Del Negro for this
  book), 19–21
The Great Big Enormous Turnip (Tolstoi),
  3, 8, 11
The Great Race (O'Malley), 43
Greek Myths (Coolidge), 114
Greene, Ellin, 8, 151
Grimm Brothers, 42, 70
Grimm's Fairy Stories, 140
*Grimms' Tales for Young and Old: The
  Complete Stories* (Manheim),
  114
Gruelle, John B., 140

H

Haase, Donald, 155
Hale, Shannon, 114
Halliwell, James Orchard, 25

Hamilton, Edith, 115
Hamilton, Martha, 80
Hamilton, Virginia, 81
"Hansel and Gretel," 34
The Hare and the Tortoise and Other Fables of La Fontaine (La Fontaine), 43
Harris, Joel Chandler, 116
Haven, Kendall, 155
Haviland, Virginia, 34, 42, 94, 152, 155
Hawes, Alison, 42
Hayes, Joe, 42
Hearne, Betsy, 151, 153, 155
The Hedley Kow (retold by Janice M. Del Negro for this book), 44–48
Hennessy, B. G., 41
Hester, Denia, 18
Ho Yi the Archer and Other Classic Chinese Tales (Fu), 155
Hoberman, Mary Ann, 42
Hoena, Blake A., 42
Holt, David, 114
Honey, James A., 48
Household Stories from the Collection of the Brothers Grimm (Crane), 122
"How Thor Lost His Hammer," 105
how-and-why books for storytelling, 161–164
humor in stories, 105
The Hungry Wolf (retold by Janice M. Del Negro for this book), 21–24
"The Hunter and the Doves," 105
Hyman, Trina Schart, 32

I

I Once Was a Monkey: Stories Buddha Told (Lee), 43
initial incident, problem, or conflict, 71
international folktales, 34
introductions in stories, 70–71

J

Jack and His Comrades (retold by Janice M. Del Negro for this book), 48–56

Jack and the Beanstalk: The Graphic Novel (Hoena), 42
"Jack and the Beanstalk," 34
Jack and the Beanstalk (Walker), 43
"Jack and the Haunted House," 68
Jack Tales, 34
Jack Tales (Chase), 48
Jackie Tales (Torrence), 80
Jacobs, Joseph, 44, 107
Japanese Fairy Tales (Ozaki), 89
The Jataka, or, Stories of the Buddha's Former Births (Cowell), 27
Jiang, Ji-Li, 152, 155
Joe Cinders (Mitchell), 81
Jolley, Dan, 80
jump tales, 68, 73–74

K

Kajikawa, Kimiko, 80
Karrik, Valerian Viliamovich, 21
Keding, Dan, 152, 155
"Keewahkee" (*When the Chenoo Howls: Native American Tales of Terror*), 114
Kennedy, Patrick, 48
Kimmel, Eria A., 114
King Hairy Goat Ears (retold by Janice M. Del Negro for this book), 56–60
Kirby, Ellie, 81
Knoop, Otto, 85
Kurtz, Jane, 114
Kuykendall, Leslee Farish, 155

L

La Fontaine, Jean de, 32, 35, 36, 43
"La Muerta: Godmother Death" (*Ready-to-Tell Tales*), 114
Lang, Andrew, 56, 94
learning stories, 69
Lee, Jeanne M., 43
Legendary Fictions of the Irish Celts (Kennedy), 48
length of stories
    ages 6 to 9, 34–35

ages 9 to 12, 68

Leodhas, Sorche Nic, 115

Leslau, Wolf, 114

Lester, Julius, 152, 156

Library Service for Children (Power), 150, 156

The Lion and the Mouse (Pinkney), 18, 42

listening groups for storytelling events, list of, 5

literacy skills, acquiring, 33

Little Red Riding Hood (Hyman), 32

Little Red Riding Hood (Marshall), 6, 8

A Little Story about a Big Turnip (Zunshine), 18

Liver (retold by Janice M. Del Negro for this book), 85–89

Look Back and See: Twenty Lively Tales for Gentle Tellers (MacDonald), 156

Lousy Rotten Stinkin' Grapes (Palatini), 43

Lowry, Amy, 43

loyalty and friendship in stories, 105

Lum, Kate, 18

Lunge-Larsen, Lise, 81, 152, 156

Lupton, Hugh, 152, 156

M

MacDonald, Margaret Read, 8, 18, 69, 70, 115, 151, 156, 179

The Magical Monkey King: Classic Chinese Tales (Jiang), 155

The Magic Orange Tree and Other Haitian Folktales (Wolkstein), 34, 43

The Magic Pipe: A Norse Tale (retold by Janice M. Del Negro for this book), 126–139

The Magic Porridge Pot (Galdone), 32, 42

Manheim, Ralph, 114

Marcantonio, Patricia Santos, 114

Marshall, James, 6, 8, 32

"Mary Culhane and the Dead Man" (*Goblin's Giggles and Other Stories*), 107, 114

McCaughrean, Geraldine, 115

McGill, Alice, 152, 156

McGovern, Ann, 43

McKissack, Patricia, 21, 152, 156

Medearis, Angela Shelf, 81

Medieval Tales (Westwood), 115

Mitchell, Marianne, 81

Moe, Jørgen, 12

"Molly Whuppie," 68

The Monkey, the Dog, and the Carabao (retold by Janice M. Del Negro for this book), 61–65

Mooney, Bill, 114

More English Fairy Tales (Jacobs), 44

More Russian Picture Tales (Karrik), 21

More Scary Stories to Tell in the Dark (Schwartz), 116

More Tales from Grimm (Grimm Brothers), 42

"Mr. Fox" - storycoaching example, 107–113

"Mr. Fox" (*English Fairy Tales*), 107

Mrs. Chicken and the Hungry Crocodile (Paye), 18

Multicultural Folktales: Stories to Tell Young Children, 10

Multicultural Literature for Children and Young Adults: Reflections on Critical Issues (Cai), 155

Muth, Jon, 43

"My Big Toe" (*Diane Goode's Book of Scary Stories and Songs*), 81

Mythology (Hamilton), 115

N

National Storytelling Network, 153

negative views of folktales, 152

"Nesoowa and the Chenoo" (*The Serpent Slayer and Other Stories of Strong Women*), 115

Nights with Uncle Remus: Myths and Legends of the Old Plantation (Harris), 116

nine to twelve years old. *See* ages 9 to 12

Norfolk, Sherry, 8

The North Wind and the Sun: A Fable (La
Fontaine), 43
"The North Wind and the Sun" -
storycoaching example, 36–41
The North Wind and the Sun (Wildsmith),
35
Nursery Tales Around the World (Sierra),
18, 156

O

O'Connor, Grace, 1
O'Malley, Kevin, 43, 81
Ottolenghi, Carol, 18
Owen, R. Emmett, 140
Ozaki, Yea Theodora, 89

P

Palatini, Margi, 43
Palmer, Francis L., 48
participatory element in stories, 3–4,
10–12, 32
Paye, Won-Ldy, 18, 152
Peace Tales (MacDonald), 115
Peck, Jan, 18
"The Peculiar Such Thing" (*The People
Could Fly: American Black
Folktales*), 81
picture books, folktales as, 165–177
Pigling: A Cinderella Story: A Korean Tale
(Jolley), 80
Pinkney, Jerry, 18, 41, 42
play, learning through, 9–10
PLOP! Splash! A Folktale from Tibet (retold
by Janice M. Del Negro for this
book), 27–30
plot development, 71–72
Poach, Margaret, 70
popular folktales, 5
Popular Rhymes and Nursery Tales
(Halliwell), 25
Popular Tales from the Norse (Asbjørnsen
& Moe), 12
*Porch Lies: Tales of Slicksters, Tricksters,
and Other Wily Characters*
(McKissack), 156

positive views of folktales, 152
Power, Effie, 150, 156
preschoolers, visual stimulus for, 2
"The Price of Smells," 105
"The Princess on the Glass Hill," 104
public speaking, author's fear of, 1
PUBYAC electronic discussion list, 149
*Putting the World in a Nutshell: The Art of
the Formula Tale* (Dailey), 5, 7
"Pygmalion and Galatea" (*Mythology*),
115
Pyle, Katharine, 126

R

*Rabbi Harvey vs. the Wisdom Kid: A
Graphic Novel of Dueling Jewish
Folktales in the Wild West*
(Sheinkin), 115
The Race of the Birkebeiners (Lunge-
Larsen), 81
Rapunzel (Gibb), 42
Rapunzel's Revenge (Hale), 114
Ready-to-Tell Tales (Holt and Mooney),
114
Red Ridin' in the Hood and Other Cuentos
(Marcantonio), 114
The Red Hen (Emberley and Emberley),
18
researching folktales, resources for,
157–159
researching storytelling, resources for,
157–159
resources for storyteller and suggested
readings
ages 3 to 6, 17–18
ages 6 to 9, 41–43
ages 9 to 12, 80–81
ages 12 to 14, 114–115
"Respect the Source: Reducing Cultural
Chaos in Picture Books, Part
Two" (*School Library Journal*),
155
romantic stories, 104
Russian Folk Tales (Afanasyev), 19
Russiche Märchen, 94

S

Sawyer, Ruth, 8, 151, 156
Sayers, Frances Clarke, 9
Schiefner, Anton, 27
Schwartz, Alvin, 116
Seale, Doris, 156
"The Sea Captain's Wife" (*Twelve Great Black Cats and Other Eerie Scottish Tales*), 115
The Serpent Slayer and Other Stories of Strong Women (Tchana), 6, 8, 115
17 U.S.C. Sect. 107, 7
17 U.S.C. Sect. 110(1), 7
Sharpe, Leah Marinsky, 81
Sheinkin, Steve, 115
Shepard, Aaron, 33
Shub, Elizabeth, 80
Sierra, Judy, 10, 18, 43, 70, 151, 156
Simon, Kristin K., 115
A Sip of Aesop (Yolen), 35, 43
six to nine years old. *See* ages 6 to 9
Slapin, Beverly, 156
Sneed, Brad, 35, 41
Soap! Soap! Soap! Don't Forget the Soap! An Appalachian Folktale (Birdseye), 42
South-African Folk-Tales (Honey), 48
Spiders in the Hairdo: Modern Urban Legends (Holt and Mooney), 114
Stanley, Diane, 43
Stenson, Jane, 8
Stevens, Janet, 12, 18
Stone Soup (Brown), 42
Stone Soup (McGovern), 43
Stone Soup (Muth), 43
stories retold by Janice M. Del Negro for this book
    Clever Grethel, 122–125
    The Demon Goblin of Adachigahara, 89–94
    Four Friends and a Lion, 82–85
    A Ghost Story, 116–121
    The Great Big Enormous Turnip,

        19–21
    The Hedley Kow, 44–48
    The Hungry Wolf, 21–24
    Jack and His Comrades, 48–56
    King Hairy Goat Ears, 56–60
    Liver, 85–89
    The Magic Pipe: A Norse Tale, 126–139
    The Monkey, the Dog, and the Carabao, 61–65
    PLOP! Splash! A Folktale from Tibet, 27–30
    The Teeny-Tiny Woman, 25–26
    The Wild Geese, 140–147
    To Your Good Health!, 94–102
Story Proof: The Science behind the Startling Power of Story (Haven), 150, 155
storycoaching examples
    "Mr. Fox," 107–113
    "The North Wind and the Sun," 36–41
    overview, 6
    "Tailypo, a Jump Tale," 73–80
    "The Three Billy Goats Gruff," 12–17
The Storyteller's Research Guide: Folktales, Myths, and Legends (Sierra), 70
The Storyteller's Sourcebook (MacDonald), 70, 179
The Storyteller's Start-Up Book: Finding, Learning, Performing and Using Folktales (MacDonald), 8, 69
storytelling. *See also* beginning storytelling books; suggested readings
    current state of, 149–154
    educational benefits of, 150
    how-and-why books for, 161–164
    overview, 4
    resources for researching, 157–159
    Web resources, 195–197
Storytelling: Art and Technique (Greene and Del Negro), 7, 8, 33, 151
Storytelling, the Art and the Purpose (Emerson), 106

The Storytelling Classroom: Applications across the Curriculum (Norfolk, Stenson, and Williams), 7, 8
straightforward presentation of story, 106
"Strength" (*Peace Tales*), 107, 115
structure of effective oral story, 70–73
Sturn, Brian W., 155
suggested readings
  A Baker's Dozen: Thirteen Stories to Tell and Read Aloud (Davis), 155
  "The Bones of Story" (*Horn Book Magazine*), 155
  The Broken Flute: The Native Experience in Books for Children (Seale and Slapin), 156
  Can You Guess My Name: Traditional Tales Around the World (Sierra), 156
  "Cite the Source: Reducing Cultural Chaos in Picture Books, Part One" (*School Library Journal*), 155
  Earth Care: World Folktales to Talk About (MacDonald), 156
  Fairy Tales and Feminism: New Approaches (Haase), 155
  Favorite Fairy Tales Told Around the World (Haviland), 155
  The Golden Lynx and Other Tales (Baker), 154
  Ho Yi the Archer and Other Classic Chinese Tales (Fu), 155
  Library Service for Children (Power), 156
  Look Back and See: Twenty Lively Tales for Gentle Tellers (MacDonald), 156
  The Magical Monkey King: Classic Chinese Tales (Jiang), 155
  Multicultural Literature for Children and Young Adults: Reflections on Critical Issues (Cai), 155
  Nursery Tales Around the World (Sierra), 156

Porch Lies: Tales of Slicksters, Tricksters, and Other Wily Characters (McKissack), 156
"Respect the Source: Reducing Cultural Chaos in Picture Books, Part Two" (*School Library Journal*), 155
Story Proof: The Science behind the Startling Power of Story (Haven), 155
Sure as Sunrise: Stories of Bruh Rabbit and His Walkin' Talkin' Friends (McGill), 156
"Swapping Tales and Stealing Stories: The Ethics and Aesthetics of Folklore in Children's Literature" (*Library Trends*), 155
Tales of Mystery and Magic (Lupton), 156
Tales of Uncle Remus: The Adventures of Brer Rabbit (Lester), 156
Tales Our Abuelitas Told: A Hispanic Folktale Collection (Ada), 154
The Talking Tree (Baker), 154
Telling Tales (Chasse), 155
Through Indian Eyes: The Native Experience in Books for Children (Slapin and Seale), 156
The Troll with No Heart in His Body and Other Tales of Trolls from Norway (Lunge-Larsen), 156
The United States of Storytelling: Folktales and True Tales from the Western States (Keding), 155
The Way of the Storyteller (Sawyer), 156
"We Said Feminist Fairy Tales, Not Fractured Fairy Tales!" (*Children and Libraries: The Journal of the Association for Library Services to Children*), 155
Wonder Tales from Around the World (Forest), 155
Summoned by Books: Essays and Speeches, 9

supernatural or gory story
    ages 9 to 12, 73
    ages 12 to 14, 106–107
*Sure as Sunrise: Stories of Bruh Rabbit
    and His Walkin' Talkin' Friends*
    (McGill), 156
"Swapping Tales and Stealing Stories: The
    Ethics and Aesthetics of Folklore
    in Children's Literature" (*Library
    Trends*), 155
*Sword of the Samurai: Adventure Stories
    from Japan* (Kimmel), 114

T

Tailypo: A Newfangled Tall Tale
    (Medearis), 81
"Tailypo," 68
"Tailypo, a Jump Tale" - storycoaching
    example, 73–80
"Tailypo" (Torrence), 81
Tailypo! (Wahl), 81
The Tailypo: A Ghost Story (Galdone), 80
Tales from Grimm (Grimm Brothers), 42
Tales of Folk and Fairies (Pyle), 126
Tales of Mystery and Magic (Lupton),
    156
*Tales of Uncle Remus: The Adventures of
    Brer Rabbit* (Lester), 156
*Tales Our Abuelitas Told: A Hispanic
    Folktale Collection* (Ada), 154
The Talking Tree (Baker), 154
Tarnowska, Wafa, 115
Tchana, Katrin, 6, 8, 115
The Teeny-Tiny Woman (retold by Janice
    M. Del Negro for this book),
    25–26
Telling Tales (Chasse), 150, 155
There's a Princess in the Palace (Alley), 80
three to six years old. *See* ages 3 to 6
"The Three Billy Goats Gruff" -
    storycoaching example, 12–17
The Three Billy Goats Gruff (Dewan), 18
The Three Billy Goats Gruff (Galdone), 2,
    3, 8, 12, 18

*The Three Billy Goats Gruff/Los Tres
    Chivitos* (Ottolenghi), 18
The Three Billy Goats Gruff (Stevens),
    18
The Three Little Pigs, 3–4
"The Three Young Men and Death"
    (*Medieval Tales*), 115
*Through Indian Eyes: The Native
    Experience in Books for Children*
    (Slapin and Seale), 156
Tibetan Tales (Schiefner), 27
Tingle, Tim, 152
"Tipingee" (*The Magic Orange Tree*), 34
To Your Good Health! (retold by Janice
    M. Del Negro for this book),
    94–102
Tolstoi, Aleksei, 8, 18
Torrence, Jackie, 80, 81
traditional folktales, 4–5
traditional linear narrative, 70–73
*Trickster: Native American Tales, a Graphic
    Collection* (Dembicki), 6, 8, 114
*The Troll with No Heart in His Body and
    Other Tales of Trolls from Norway*
    (Lunge-Larsen), 156
Tsunami! (Kajikawa), 80
*Twelve Great Black Cats and Other Eerie
    Scottish Tales* (Leodhas), 115
twelve to fourteen years old. *See* ages 12
    to 14
*Twenty Tellable Tales: Audience
    Participation Folktales for
    the Beginning Storyteller*
    (MacDonald), 8, 33

U

The Uglified Ducky (Claflin), 42
Ungar, Richard, 81
*The United States of Storytelling: Folktales
    and True Tales from the Western
    States* (Keding), 155
*Unwitting Wisdom: An Anthology of Aesop's
    Fables* (Ward), 43

V

Valentino, Jim, 115
Vande Velde, Vivian, 115
"Vasilisa the Beautiful," 104
Velcome (O'Malley), 81
Very Short Fables to Read Together (Hoberman), 42
The Violet Fairy Book (Lang), 56
visual stimulus for preschoolers, 2

W

Wahl, Jan, 81
Walker, Richard, 43
Ward, Helen, 43
Warner, Charles Dudley, 82
Washington, Donna, 43, 81, 152
The Way of the Storyteller (Sawyer), 8, 151, 156
"We Said Feminist Fairy Tales, Not Fractured Fairy Tales!" (*Children and Libraries: The Journal of the Association for Library Services to Children*), 155
Web resources for folktales and storytelling, 195–197
Weiss, Mitch, 80
Westwood, Jennifer, 115
What! Cried Granny: An Almost Bedtime Story; A Silly, Funny Granny Tries to Put Her Grandson to Bed (Lum), 18

When the Chenoo Howls: Native American Tales of Terror (Bruchac and Bruchac), 114
The Whole Story Handbook (Birch), 70
"Why Frog and Snake Never Play Together" (*Ashley Bryan's African Tales, Uh-Huh*), 34
Wildsmith, Brian, 35
The Wild Geese (retold by Janice M. Del Negro for this book), 140–147
Wiley and the Hairy Man (Sierra), 43
Williams, Diane, 8
The Wind and the Sun (Hawes), 42
Wolkstein, Diane, 34, 43
Wonder Tales from Around the World (Forest), 155
The World's Best Literature, Volume 19 (Warner, Cunliffe, et al.), 82
"The World's Reward" (*South-African Folk-Tales*), 48

Y

Yolen, Jane, 35, 43, 152
Yummy: Eight Favorite Fairy Tales (Cousins), 17

Z

Zunshine, Tatiana, 18